# SUCCESS *AND* ITS SHADOWS

# SUCCESS *AND* ITS SHADOWS

## The Hidden Temptations Behind Every Strength and the Character That Keeps You Whole

SEBASTIAN VADUVA, PHD

*Success and Its Shadows*
by Sebastian Vaduva, PhD



Printed in the United States of America

ISBN: 978-1-962802-67-3.



High Bridge Books titles may be purchased in bulk for educational, business, fundraising, or sales promotional use. For information, please contact High Bridge Books via www.HighBridgeBooks.com/contact.

Published in Houston, Texas, by High Bridge Books.

*To my daughter, Evelina Delia—*
*Dare to do great things with God!*

# ACKNOWLEDGMENTS

THIS PROJECT HAS BEEN MADE POSSIBLE BY THE generous financial support of Marcus Sebastian BUNTA of https://marcussebastianrenovations.com/

Further support has been provided by the following individuals:

> Lois Văduva, Aurel Mureșan, Dan Eberhart, Alin Mercheș, Ana Giurcă, Samson Popescu, Cornel Mihai, Silviu Isidor, Nelu Bălan, Călin Farcău, Dan Schipor, Dan Dărăban, Dacian Lontiș, Narcis Ranghiuc, Ionuț Breb, Cătălin Vasilovici, Beniamin Clapa, Beniamin Urs, Claudiu Dan, Cosmin Nagi, Mihai Doci, Nelu Sigartău, Ștefan Pastia, Tudor Cioflică, Gaius Văduva, asociația Integrity business Club Timișoara, Vasilica Zuld, Gaius Vaduva, Luca Daniela-Diana, Elton Sayani, Daniel Burtic, Claudia Mariana Săuciuc; Laviniu Gabor, Vlad Mihuț, Marius-Bogdan Fiț, Nicu Munteanu, Adrei Stroca, Bogdan Toader, Cristian Pătrașcu, Johnny- Ionut Neacsu, Ioan & Ciprian Bențe, and Dan Copăcean

# CONTENTS

# PREFACE

IN THE WINTER OF 1999, I WAS A YOUNG BUSINESS PROFESSOR at the University of Akron when I received an invitation that would change the course of my teaching and thinking. Emanuel University in Oradea, Romania, had just launched a business school, and its leaders invited me to speak with their students. I was deeply honored but also a bit terrified. I was only 23 years old at that time and did not feel prepared to speak about business and capitalism to students full of questions who lived in a post-Communist society.

During a conversation with Dr. Paul Negruț, the university's president, he advised, "Why don't you put together materials based on the books and experiences that have shaped your life?" John Lenton, the founder of the university's business school, added, "Think about the principles and practices that shaped America. Tell our students how a former British colony rose to become a world leader." At the time, barely a decade after the fall of Communism, the story of America's economic and cultural rise held an enormous fascination for Romania. Dr. Negruț's and Lenton's advice gave me direction. I decided to build the course around the very ideas they highlighted: the books that had formed me, the principles that undergird American success, and the lessons emerging leaders in Eastern Europe needed most. Their guidance became the foundation of my approach to teaching leadership and entrepreneurship in a society still searching for models of freedom, initiative, and responsibility.

The content I developed for those initial lectures eventually became an organizational behavior course I still teach today. Over the years, this course has provided the foundation for my public lectures, corporate training sessions, and TV/radio appearances. This book is the culmination of that journey, one that began in the late 1990s and continues to evolve with every generation of students and business professionals I've had the privilege to teach.

For a long time, however, I felt the course was missing something. The course explained how successful societies function, but it did not yet fully address why some people and organizations thrive while others stagnate. I needed a deeper, more lived perspective on resilience, character, and calling. That clarity came during the COVID-19 pandemic.

With everything shut down in Romania, my family and I spent the 2020–2021 academic year in Austin, Texas. It was one of the most difficult and beautiful seasons of our lives. Due to the time difference, we taught our Romanian students online starting at 4 a.m. In the evenings, I taught in-person MBA classes at Concordia University Texas.

Amid that demanding schedule, we found a spiritual home at Park Hills Church in Austin, pastored by a dear friend and fellow Romanian, Samuel Viorel Clintoc. During that year, his sermons focused on the book of 1 Samuel in the Old Testament, exploring the contrasting leadership styles of kings Saul and David. Though I was familiar with the biblical narrative, I began to see how these ancient lessons applied directly to my organizational behavior course. Teaching about success without addressing its dangers and temptations was incomplete. My course was already emphasizing business and life success, and it was grounded in ethics and Christian values. However, after Austin, I understood the inherent dangers of success and that, as with King Saul, success without vigilance leads to downfall. I realized that every trademark of successful people has a corresponding temptation. True success requires an awareness of that reality, along with a strategy to enhance the success characteristic and neutralize its temptations.

## What Inspired This Book?

One of the key influences behind my work is Niall Ferguson's book, *Civilization: The West and the Rest*. Ferguson explores prosperity from a historical and macroeconomic perspective, and his conclusions are sobering. Looking back across almost 10,000 years of recorded history, human experience has been marked by suffering. Natural disasters like famine, disease, drought, and floods—along with manmade horrors such as wars, slavery, and oppressions—were the norm. Tragically, more than half the world's population still lives in such conditions today.

The notable exceptions? The West: Europe and the United States for the last four centuries. While far from perfect and sometimes hypocritical, Western societies have achieved undeniable success. Since the 16th century, spiritual renewal and cultural transformation have fueled innovations in agriculture, medicine, economics, science, politics, and governance. Today, the quality of life enjoyed by even the poorest person in the West far exceeds that of royalty just a few centuries ago.

Ferguson argues that this progress stems from the Judeo-Christian foundation of Western culture, especially its emphasis on *restraint,* which is the idea that reason and the **will**—not wild passions and desires—should govern behavior. This ethic promoted responsibility, delayed gratification, and hard work—values that fueled both moral and economic development.

However, since the mid-20th century, the West has slowly abandoned that formula for success. Instead of responsibility and self-denial, we've embraced a distorted version of freedom. Ferguson points to Sigmund Freud and modern psychology as a pivotal influence in this cultural shift. His emphasis on self-expression, pleasure, and misunderstood freedom laid the groundwork for a society more concerned with rights than responsibilities. The result? A decline in work ethic, the rise of entitlement, and a belief that success should come through protest and redistribution rather than from discipline and sacrifice.

As I will explain in this book, I do not deny the West's failures, but I reject the idea that tearing down its values is the answer. Real change begins at the individual level—when we embrace our gifts, recognize our context, and commit to a life of hard work and character.

## Who Is This Book For?

While I believe this book can benefit anyone, I had three specific audiences in mind as I wrote it:

1. **Young adults** – High school and college students: You're at a pivotal stage in life. The habits you form now will shape your future. My hope is that this book will equip you with timeless principles for building a successful life and career.
2. **Parents and grandparents** – You are the most important educators in a young person's life. I hope this book becomes a conversation starter in your home. Don't outsource the responsibility of teaching and mentoring to schools and teachers. Invest time and wisdom in your children and grandchildren.
3. **Seasoned professionals seeking meaning** – If you've achieved success and are now wondering what it all means, this book is also for you. Consider using it in mentorship groups or book clubs where you can pass along what you've learned while continuing your own journey of growth.

## What Makes This Book Unique?

This book is shaped by three key elements:

1. **Blend of academic rigor and real-world practice** – I've studied success from both scholarly and popular sources, but I've also lived it in classrooms, companies, and conversations. Theory without practice is useless, and practice without theory is blind. True wisdom lies in the intertwining of theory with practice.

2. **Cross-cultural perspective** – I've had the privilege of living, studying, and working in both Romania (representing the East) and the United States (representing the West). Both contain unique perspectives, and I believe their integration can offer a powerful blueprint for success.
3. **Christian foundation** – While I respect all beliefs, my personal convictions are Christian, and they shape the heart of this book. I do not want to proselytize but to offer a holistic vision of success—one that addresses both the virtues and the vices that come with it. Too many books either celebrate success without acknowledging its dangers or critique business success without offering solutions. I believe we can and must pursue both success and integrity.

## Structure of the Book

This book is divided into eight chapters. In the first chapter, I lay out my understanding of success. Each of the subsequent seven chapters explores a key trait essential for success, the temptation that is usually associated with it, and several strategies for overcoming that temptation. The seven trademarks and corresponding temptations I have identified among successful people are as follows:

| Trademarks of successful people | Temptations of successful people |
|---|---|
| Natural talents | Pride |
| Persuasiveness | Dishonesty |
| Industriousness | Materialism |
| Creativity | Discontentment |
| Determination | Anger |
| Altruism | Revenge |
| Pragmatism | Superficiality |

Each chapter seeks to help readers cultivate these success characteristics while guarding against the temptations that could destroy them. My hope is that this book will not only be a guide to achievement but also a companion in the lifelong journey toward meaningful, ethical, and enduring success. The elevator to success is broken; you must take the stairs!

# Introduction

# THE STRENGTHS AND SHADOWS OF SUCCESS

*Every strength contains a shadow, and true success requires cultivating the strength while restraining its corresponding temptation.*

SUCCESS HAS FASCINATED ME FOR AS LONG AS I CAN remember. Growing up in a poor family in communist Romania, I experienced material scarcity firsthand. At the time, I believed success meant having enough food, warmth, and access to good TV programs. As I grew older, my definition shifted. Because my father often shamed us through his violence and alcoholism, I began to see success as gaining the respect of the community. At age 12, my family emigrated to the United States, where I assumed material security and social acceptance would follow naturally. Having been raised in the bleak landscape of communism, I imagined America as a land without struggles. That illusion shattered just three months after arriving in Chicago, when my father abandoned us. Suddenly, survival became my new definition of success. My mother, my two siblings, and I were left to navigate a foreign country without knowing the language or culture.

In the U.S., I encountered a new vision of success—one shaped by materialism and larger-than-life figures like John D. Rockefeller, Bill Gates, and Steve Jobs. I devoured books by Zig Ziglar, Horatio Alger, Brian Tracy, and John Maxwell, all of whom preached the gospel of success. At 17, determined to chase the *American Dream,* I started my first business—a butcher shop. Because I was too young to sign any contracts, I secured a loan in my mother's name. At that stage, success meant selling as much as possible, to as many people as possible, and as often as possible to maximize my profit.

My days would start at 4 a.m. at the shop, followed by school and later college. By 1998, I had begun my MBA at one of the most prestigious business schools in the country, and my ambition had crystallized: I would become the CEO of a Fortune 500 company before turning 35.

But what is success, really? My journey—from scarcity to survival and from entrepreneurship to corporate ambition—has shown me that success is more than just material gain. It is a constantly evolving pursuit, shaped by experience, hardship, and personal decisions. In the early 1990s, ABC aired a Barbara Walters special called *The Shame of a Nation*, exposing the horrific conditions of Romanian orphanages, the nation my family had just escaped a few years earlier. Watching the plight of those orphans shook me to my core. Until that moment, I had seen myself as unlucky, maybe even cursed, to have been born into a large, poor family with an alcoholic father. My classmates were financially secure, while I had to borrow money and work in a freezing butcher shop. I felt like just another immigrant, barely tolerated in America.

However, compared to those Romanian orphans, I was a prince. I lived in a wealthy country, surrounded by opportunity. As I sat there watching the documentary, I felt a whisper in my heart: *Aren't you blessed to be here in America? Perhaps you are in a position to help those children. Stop feeling sorry for yourself!*

That moment redefined success for me—again. While I remained deeply committed to entrepreneurship, I realized my goal was no longer just to build wealth for myself. My definition of success had become helping as many people as possible. My MBA colleagues pursued high-powered consulting careers at firms like McKinsey, but through a series of unexpected, divinely orchestrated events, I became a professor at the University of Akron. That prepared me for the next stage of my life, returning to Romania in 2004. Here, I've had the privilege of training more than 10,000 students, managers, and entrepreneurs. I've advised over 50 companies and participated in more than 25 startups with various partners and collaborators. The lessons I have learned and the people I have observed, combined with my academic research, are encapsulated in this book. While it may be a limited and personal perspective, I trust my experiences and insights will serve as a guide on your own journey to success.

## Success: The Desire of the Soul

Success is a universal pursuit, yet its definition remains elusive. We see it echoed in countless quotes:

> "Success is not final; failure is not fatal: it is the courage to continue that counts." —Winston Churchill

> "Try not to become a man of success but rather try to become a man of value." —Albert Einstein

> "Success is getting what you want. Happiness is wanting what you get." —Dale Carnegie

> "I succeed because I believe I can." —paraphrased from Virgil

Regardless of whether you've heard these exact quotes, they all attempt to capture the essence of success. Since childhood, most of us have been conditioned to chase success—whether it is earning good grades in school, securing the right job, building a thriving business, or planning a picture-perfect wedding. Society showcases success through larger-than-life figures, making it seem both enviable and essential. We wish each other "good luck" before an exam, job interview, or a major purchase, reinforcing the idea that success is both desirable and necessary.

I have met countless individuals who initially defined success a certain way, achieved it, felt unfulfilled, and then changed their definition. Some believed graduating from college would give them satisfaction; they did graduate but remained dissatisfied. Others thought marriage would bring them success, but soon after the wedding, they were disappointed or worse, convinced they had made the wrong choice. Some equated success with landing a good job, moving to a different country or city, starting a business, taking an exotic vacation, or building the house of their dreams. Still, fulfillment eluded them. I won't attempt to offer a rigid or universal definition of success because I believe success is inherently unique and personal.

I will only offer behavioral tools that support a successful life. Based on personal experience and research, I've identified seven general traits that can be cultivated to achieve success:

1. Natural talents
2. Persuasiveness
3. Industriousness
4. Creativity
5. Determination
6. Altruism
7. Pragmatism

Regardless of your particular calling or set of gifts, I believe these characteristics can help guide you on your journey. While the importance of each trademark may vary from person to person and from situation to situation, they are all valuable.

To be sure, possessing these traits does not automatically or effortlessly lead you to success. In fact, many people who naturally possess these traits disregard them and never get around to using them. However, based on my experience and research, without them, success is often difficult—if not impossible—to attain. The good news is that, regardless of your background and DNA, with the help of God, these traits can be cultivated. In the subsequent chapters, I will offer practical strategies to enhance these characteristics and encourage you to seek out role models and additional information to help you become what God meant you to be.

## Each strength of successful people comes with a corresponding temptation/shadow.

However, every strength contains a shadow, and true success requires cultivating the strength while restraining its corresponding temptation. You can observe this most vividly in individuals who are naturally endowed with these characteristics but ruin their lives because they cannot rule over their demons. Thankfully, these temptations are not inevitable and can be overcome, but we must be aware of them and develop appropriate mechanisms to keep them in check. Unfortunately, on this side of heaven, I do not believe we can eliminate our temptations entirely.

While hundreds, if not thousands, of books, articles, podcasts, and videos explore success, few address the powerful and subtle temptations that come with it. Even fewer examine the connection between these temptations and the very traits that enable our success. The challenge for us is to develop the characteristics that yield success continuously, while neutralizing the temptations that can deceive us so easily. In the subsequent chapters, I will present a success characteristic along with the corresponding temptation, its manifestations and dangers, and offer practical recommendations to neutralize it.

While this book does not attempt to define success in a single, rigid way, it does aim to lay a foundation for deeper reflection. By examining both the traits that lead to success and the temptations that threaten it, my goal is not to provide dogmatic answers but to spark meaningful conversation and personal growth. True success is more than just achievement—it is a journey of wisdom, integrity, and purpose. Let's explore it together!

## Success Is Subjective

The first point I want to stress is that success is subjective to each individual.[1] Solomon the Wise said,

> The race is not to the swift, nor the battle to the strong, nor bread to the wise, nor riches to men of understanding, nor favor to men of skill; but time and chance happen to them all.

This is not a fatalistic statement meant to imply that we have no influence over our own success. Instead, it constructively invites us to understand and build success within the framework of our individual contexts. Each person has a unique set of circumstances, making their definition of success deeply personal and subjective. Just as no two people have identical fingerprints, no two individuals share the exact same path to fulfillment. Our uniqueness is formed by countless factors—family, background, culture, personality, desires, dreams, and experiences—all of which shape how we define and pursue success.

Naturally, there are dangers in subjectivism. Perhaps you've heard someone say, "You're being too subjective; you need to be more objective." Indeed, there are moments when objectivity is critical—such as in justice, decision-making, or conflict resolution. I've encountered many people who believe they are successful, yet most people around them do not see it. These individuals are not successful; they may be trapped in self-delusion. Subjectivity becomes dangerous when it's used to justify selfish or harmful decisions.

---

[1] Nash, L., & Stevenson, H. (2004). Success that lasts. *Harvard Business Review,* 82(2), 102–109.

When it comes to success, however, subjectivism can be reframed as uniqueness. Each of us has been uniquely gifted and placed in distinct circumstances. Therefore, success does not have a one-size-fits-all definition; it is a personal and individualized concept. A humorous story illustrates this point well.

> Two prisoners on death row were given their last wish. In a melancholic voice, the first one said, "If I could only listen to country music one last time ..." Panicked, the second prisoner blurted, "Please, execute me first! I'd rather die than listen to country music one more time."

Our subjectivity is grounded in our values, priorities, and DNA. Each of us has different goals, which means our visions for success will vary. For one person, success may mean owning a house and a car. For another, it may be building a happy family or accumulating wealth. Personality also plays a crucial role. An extrovert may equate success with public recognition as a performer or a leader, while an introvert may define success as quietly developing innovations or working independently.

Values, shaped by our upbringing and life experiences, guide our goals and the methods by which we pursue them. Some people value freedom and define success as the ability to travel. Others prize stability and associate success with building a strong, enduring career. Someone who values integrity will pursue success through ethical means.

In this context, subjectivism is not a weakness but a strength. Our individual uniqueness makes our paths to success diverse but also complementary, like puzzle pieces coming together to form a beautiful picture. When we appreciate and collaborate with others, we enrich the collective pursuit of fulfillment.[2]

---

[2] Ng, T. W. H., Eby, L. T., Sorensen, K. L., & Feldman, D. C. (2005). Predictors of objective and subjective career success: A meta-analysis. *Personnel Psychology, 58*(2), 367–408. https://doi.org/10.1111/j.1744-6570.2005.00515.

## Success Is Contentment

To avoid disillusionment, the key is not to have what you want but to want what you have. This does not mean abandoning ambition; it means learning the art of contentment. It is entirely possible to reach your goals and still feel dissatisfied. Without contentment, life becomes a constant, exhausting pursuit of more. In my research and experience, I've seen many people chase success without ever defining it. As human beings, we are easily influenced. We see someone with a certain job or car and assume their happiness comes from those things. This is the engine behind advertising: it fuels our dissatisfaction, envy, and relentless desire for more. We must have the courage to define our individual definition of success and patiently work toward it, fully aware that there will be setbacks along the way.

## Success Can Be Denigrated

You may be familiar with the fables of Aesop, who taught life lessons through animal characters. One such fable tells of a fox who sees a bunch of grapes hanging on a vine. Hungry, he leaps again and again to reach them but fails. Eventually, he gives up and mutters bitterly, "Those grapes were sour anyway." Many people adopt a similar attitude. They desire success but are not willing to work hard for it and make the necessary sacrifices. Like the fox, they tell themselves and others that success is not worth the effort or that the system is rigged anyway.

An uncomfortable yet important reality is the human tendency to denigrate the success of others when they have not achieved it themselves. This attitude can take many forms, from undervaluing others' accomplishments to justifying our own failures and pointing to the "unfairness" of the system. This denigration can be manifested in several ways:

1. **Trivializing achievements** – "Yes, he won the award, but he probably had connections," or "Anyone could've done it if they had the resources."
2. **Attributing success to external factors** – "He was lucky to be in the right place at the right time," or "His wealthy parents are responsible for his success."
3. **Focusing on flaws** – Obsessing over small mistakes or imperfections in successful individuals while ignoring the broader scope of their achievements.
4. **Resignation** – "The system is rigged anyway. Only the corrupt make it to the top."
5. **Redefining success to fit one's own attitude** – "Sure, he has money, but I bet he doesn't have a fulfilling personal life," or "True success isn't measured in money or fame."

Some people become so critical of success that they glorify failure or poverty in an unhealthy way. They claim they don't want material success, not out of conviction or calling but from an arrogant motivation. They come to see themselves as better or holier than the rich, taking pride in not being like "those materialists."

One troubling pattern I've noticed is that this denigration often masks comfort seeking or even laziness. As we'll explore in upcoming chapters, success demands hard work and resilience. If you want to succeed, the question isn't *if* you'll fail but *when* you'll fail and what you'll do afterward. Sometimes, those downplaying success are not willing to get up and try again after repeated failures.

People who belittle success are often hypocritical. Outwardly, they claim not to want the material or social rewards that come with success, but secretly, they desire them intensely. Their hope is to gain these rewards by luck, the lottery, or some kind of cosmic shortcut, without putting in the effort and exposing themselves to the certainty of failure along the way. The truth is they want to be successful, both materially and socially, but do not want to discipline themselves and experience the uncomfortable process of achieving success.

## The Components of Success

### *Material Well-Being*

The first component of success, which is often misunderstood due to its abuse, is material well-being. I have seen two extremes, both equally dangerous. On one extreme, people consider success exclusively in terms of money and material possessions. To them, being successful means being wealthy—nothing more, nothing less. These people think they can buy anything with money, and they seem to concern themselves only with accumulating material possessions. This definition of success is presented by the media and exemplified by the so-called success stories in our society.

At the other extreme is the notion that success and fulfillment are best achieved through poverty. In this view, to be pure at heart, you must not concern yourself with worldly possessions; instead, you should focus on meaning well. Those who adhere to this extreme seem to be spending all their time talking about what's wrong in the world and think that if they complain loudly enough or nasty enough about the wrongs of society, they will magically fix themselves somehow.

Both extremes can be dangerous, and you must figure out how to balance both to be successful. I have noticed that material well-being is an important component of a successful life, without which many initiatives can be curtailed. There are two major components every person should be aware of: *periodic income* and *net worth*.

Periodic income[3] refers to the steady flow of cash that supports daily living. It might come from a salary, investment income,

---

[3] Koh, B. (2012). *Personal financial planning*. FT Press.

dividends, or business profits. It provides the stability needed to cover current expenses, invest in personal and professional growth, and seize new opportunities. A strong and diversified income stream brings not just material comfort but also the freedom to make choices without being shackled by financial pressure. It enables people to take calculated risks, pursue goals, and grow.

Net worth is the long-term measure of financial health and includes assets like real estate, stock portfolios, business interests, and possessions such as cars, properties, etc.

Net worth reflects long-term financial independence and sustainability. While periodic income provides short-term comfort, net worth ensures long-term security and the possibility of leaving a legacy. It grants access to investment opportunities, serves as a buffer against economic instability, and has the potential to make earning periodic income optional. High net worth can be leveraged for large-scale philanthropy and meaningful societal impact. While periodic income is the engine of daily financial success, net worth is the foundation on which lasting financial success and legacy are built.

However, wealth is not a destination; it's only a tool for pursuing something greater, such as personal growth, impact, fulfillment, and legacy. Financial resources empower us to reach higher goals, enrich relationships, and contribute meaningfully to society. Money gives us freedom and flexibility but should never overshadow what matters most: our spiritual well-being, physical health, relationships, character, and faith. It has been said, "Money is a great servant, but a terrible master." If money becomes your master, then the love of money will cloud your judgment and distort your priorities. And even if you do attain it, there's no guarantee it will last.

At the same time, we all recognize the limitations of poverty: you can't pay bills, travel, care for your family, or invest in growth. So money is not to be avoided—quite the opposite. Success requires some level of financial independence. This doesn't mean becoming rich but rather gaining the stability to make value-driven decisions without financial constraints.

Financial independence can empower you to pursue your calling, take career risks, and avoid soul-draining compromises. It reduces stress and frees up energy for long-term goals. It also enables you to say "no" to opportunities that aren't aligned with your purpose.

Money should not determine your direction—only your speed. Your direction is set by your calling—by what you feel compelled to do. If you have resources, you may reach your destination faster. If not, you'll still get there—just more slowly. Sadly, I've met many who dream big but never crunch the numbers. When the time comes to implement their ideas, they face financial shortfalls and are forced to compromise or even stop. Every dream, vision, and plan needs a realistic financial strategy. Otherwise, disappointment replaces enthusiasm, and frustration replaces vision.

### *Respect and Influence*

Respect and influence are powerful indicators of authentic and lasting success. They reflect not only what we've achieved but *who we are* and *what impact we've made*. It is beautiful when people look at your life and see you as a role model.

Respect—especially from your family—is never an automatic gift. It is earned through consistency, integrity, and excellence in your craft. When we are respected, our words carry weight, our presence brings value, and doors open. Respect creates trust, forges deep relationships, and lays the groundwork for sustainable success.

Influence is the ability to lead others through example. When others look to us as sources of inspiration, we contribute to a better world. Influence takes many forms: mentoring the next generation, leading public discourse, or catalyzing social reform. But genuine influence isn't about manipulation or power—it's about connection, purpose, and shared values.

History is full of people who made a profound impact without personal wealth—because they were respected and supported by those who had it. Consider the Medici family during the Italian Renaissance. Their financial support enabled geniuses like Leonardo da Vinci and Michelangelo to devote themselves to art and innovation. Da Vinci pursued groundbreaking work. Michelangelo created timeless masterpieces like the Sistine Chapel ceiling. The Medicis didn't just fund talent; they shaped history.

We see this same pattern today in elite institutions. Universities like Harvard support researchers and creatives so they can focus on their work without financial worry.

In our digital age, respect and influence have expanded. A meaningful online presence and thoughtful content can now build global influence.[4] But with influence comes responsibility—to use that influence wisely, ethically, and constructively.

Respect and influence can't be forced. They're earned through a life of purpose, integrity, and service. Real success isn't just about personal advancement; it's about elevating others, taking responsibility for your impact, and striving to be the best version of yourself.

Ultimately, to be respected and influential is to have the power to shape the future—not just your own future but also the future of those around you. This is perhaps the deepest and most fulfilling form of success: to leave a positive, enduring legacy that empowers others to reach their potential and serve the greater good.

### *Family Harmony*

Family plays a crucial role in our success in many ways. When I refer to "family," I am speaking about the inner circle, that sacred corner of life built by you, your spouse, and your children. I'm not referring to grandparents, parents, in-laws, uncles, aunts, or siblings. In my experience, the extended family often has its own agenda for your life, and its members carry strong opinions. While I do not advocate

---

[4] Leung, F. F., Gu, F. F., & Palmatier, R. W. (2022). Online influencer marketing. *Journal of the Academy of Marketing Science, 50*(2), 226–251. https://doi.org/10.1007/s11747-021-00806-3.

indifference toward relatives, it's important to acknowledge they can sometimes exert a negative influence on our lives and decisions. They may pressure us into thinking and acting in ways that align with their own values and expectations, even when we are called to a different path.

Family, then, is deeply tied to our success. Even in movies like *The Godfather*, the protagonists—though criminals—earned respect, admiration, and influence largely by being portrayed as devoted family men. There is something inherently respectable about being a family person. It's not uncommon to hear someone say, "He's a stand-up guy, a good family man." This statement carries a sense of respect and admiration, often reflecting a deeper cultural value placed on family. In many American communities, especially within more traditional or conservative circles, being recognized as a man or woman devoted to family suggests stability, responsibility, and moral integrity.

One of the greatest temptations we face in life is selfishness, which inevitably breeds discontent. Learning how to curb our selfish impulses is mandatory in our quest to live successful lives. I believe that God placed us in families precisely to confront and restrain our selfishness. Unhappy families are often made up of selfish individuals who are frustrated that others do not meet their needs. In contrast, happy families consist of altruistic individuals committed to meeting each other's needs. It may sound paradoxical, but it is profoundly true: it is more blessed to give than to receive. Within the family, we have the best opportunity to practice altruism. In doing so, we cultivate both happiness and success.

Unfortunately, in the relentless pursuit of professional and financial success, many fall into the trap of neglecting their families, wrongly viewing them as barriers to personal advancement. They pour their time and energy into their careers, believing that present sacrifices will yield future rewards. Yet this mindset is deeply flawed and often leads to devastating consequences.

Family is not a hindrance to success; it is a solid foundation that provides the emotional stability and moral support necessary to face life's challenges. Neglecting these relationships can lead to alienation, conflict, and ultimately a profound sense of emptiness and regret. True success cannot be measured solely by career milestones or material gains; it must also include the quality of one's personal relationships.

A strong, close-knit family creates a loving, supportive, and nurturing environment that is essential for both personal growth and professional development. Maintaining a healthy work-life balance allows us to sustain long-term motivation and avoid burnout. That's why it's vital to invest time and energy in building and strengthening family ties. They are not peripheral to success; they are central to it. Lasting success and true happiness are built on the foundation of meaningful, loving relationships.

### *Inner Peace*

Mark Twain famously said, "The two most important days in your life are the day you are born and the day you find out why you were born." Understanding the "why" of our existence is what separates truly successful people from those who simply drift through life. Those who live with purpose, who wake up each day knowing that their life has meaning beyond the immediate tasks in front of them, tend to have an inner peace that fuels resilience, focus, and fulfillment. This kind of peace cannot be fabricated by external success or bought with wealth. It is anchored in identity—knowing who you are, whose you are, and why you're here. Without that grounding, even the most impressive achievements can feel hollow. We see this in the lives of many celebrities, high-powered executives, and public figures who seem to have it all yet suffer from burnout, addiction, or depression. Their outer success masks inner emptiness.

As Christians, we believe that our identity and purpose are rooted in God. We are not random products of chance or ambition. We were created for a reason that goes beyond ourselves. When we align our lives with God's calling, we tap into a source of peace that doesn't waver with circumstances. Jesus said, "Peace I leave with you; my peace I give you. I do not give to you as the world gives" (John 14:27). This peace, His peace, is not fragile. It does not depend on promotions, applause, or possessions. It endures.

This is why inner peace is essential to lasting success. It gives us perspective. It reminds us that we are more than our titles and paychecks. It protects us from the toxic drive to prove our worth through achievement, and it allows us to endure hardships with grace because we know our lives are part of a bigger story—God's story.

People without inner peace often chase success compulsively. They may accomplish a great deal, but they are driven by fear, insecurity, or the need to impress others. Their success feels frantic, restless, and unsustainable. In contrast, when you operate from a place of inner peace, your work becomes an expression of who you are rather than a desperate attempt to define yourself. You're able to say no to things that don't align with your purpose and yes to the things that do, even if they seem less impressive in the eyes of others.

---

*There is a common misconception that success is merely a result of luck. Yet, for every "lucky" individual, there are at least five others with equal talent who never fully realize their potential.*

---

Success without peace is not success at all. Inner peace grounds us, guides us, and frees us to live authentically. It is cultivated in the quiet moments: in prayer, reflection, Scripture reading, meaningful conversation, and acts of love. It grows when we live in harmony with our values and in surrender to God's will.

If you're serious about real success, start by asking deeper questions: Who am I? Why am I here? What has God called me to do in this season of my life? The answers may not come all at once, but the pursuit of those answers will lead you to a peace that success alone could never provide.

Each person has been created by God for a unique purpose. God is a good and sovereign Creator who has designed meaningful plans for our lives. However, He also allows challenges and hardships, not as punishments but as opportunities to shape our character. The essence of success lies in accepting this divine plan, even when life seems unfair.

Faith provides the strength to work, grow, and persevere—not out of revenge or bitterness but out of peace and confidence. When you believe that your life has a divine purpose, you will no longer wander aimlessly. Instead, you will move forward with certainty, knowing that a perfect plan has already been designed by a good and loving God.

## The Road to Success

Wanting to be successful is a good thing. In fact, simply being interested in this subject is the first step on the path to success. However, most people desire success, yet few take the necessary steps, persist through challenges, and maintain their commitment long enough to achieve their vision.

Those who attain lasting success build it on a solid foundation. In the following chapters, I will introduce seven key principles that can help lay this foundation. This book will explore what it truly means to be successful, not just in wealth or status but in character and purpose. We will examine the essential traits of success as well as the temptations and obstacles that can lead us astray. With a firm foundation, you will be equipped to overcome these challenges and pursue a life of true fulfillment.

---

*If you are a gifted person, it does not mean that you have won something; it means that you have something to give back.*

— CARL JUNG

---

## Further Reading

Acemoglu, D., & Robinson, J. A. (2012). *Why nations fail: The origins of power, prosperity, and poverty*. Crown Business.

Bufford, B. (1994). *Halftime: Moving from success to significance*. Zondervan.

Clason, G. S. (2008). *The richest man in Babylon*. Signet.

Geisler, N. L., & Hoffman, P. K. (2001). *Why I am a Christian: Leading thinkers explain why they believe*. Baker Books.

Graham, B. (2003). *Peace with God: The secret of happiness*. Thomas Nelson.

Huffington, A. (2014). *Thrive: The third metric to redefining success and creating a life of well-being, wisdom, and wonder*. Harmony Books.

Jaku, E. (2020). *The happiest man on Earth: The beautiful life of an Auschwitz survivor*. Pan Macmillan.
(*Note: Subtitle may vary slightly across editions; original Australian title used here.*)

Lennox, J. C. (2021). *God's gravedigger: Has science buried God?* Christian Focus Publications.

Lutzer, E. W. (2015). *Seven reasons why you can trust the Bible*. Moody Publishers.

Mate, G., & Neufeld, G. (2005). *Hold on to your kids: Why parents need to matter more than peers*. Ballantine Books.

Negruț, P. (2007.). *It is not good for man to be alone: Theological and psychological perspectives on the family*. Emanuel University Press.

Steiger, A. (2021). *Reclaimed: How Jesus Restores Our Humanity in a Dehumanized World*. Apologetics Canada.

# 1

# NATURAL TALENTS VS. PRIDE

SUCCESS AND FAILURE OFTEN HINGE ON HOW WE recognize and develop our natural talents. In this chapter, we explore the natural gifts that contribute to success and how individuals can capitalize on them. However, with success comes the ever-present temptation of pride, which can have detrimental effects. While we cannot account for every human talent or circumstance, our goal is to highlight key principles of success and how to apply them in our own lives.

## Natural Talents That Contribute to Success

The following attributes are among the most influential in shaping one's path to success.

### *Energy*

Physical, mental, and spiritual energy drive human activity. Some individuals possess seemingly boundless energy. They require less sleep, work harder and faster, and maintain a resilient attitude. Their vitality is evident in their speech, their walk, and their approach to challenges. Mental energy enables them to recover quickly from setbacks, and spiritual energy allows them to connect with others on a deeper level.

However, those blessed with high energy must be cautious not to waste it on distractions. Without discipline, their vigor can be scattered, leading to exhaustion rather than productivity.

### *Physical Appearance*

In an age dominated by social media, physical appearance is often overemphasized as a determinant of success. While first impressions matter and people are naturally drawn to attractiveness, relying solely on looks is a precarious strategy.

Those who prioritize appearance above all else may neglect other essential skills, and those who feel they lack beauty may become insecure or envious. True success comes from a balanced approach: caring for one's appearance and hygiene while cultivating kindness and character, the real sources of charm.

### *Memory*

A strong memory has historically been a hallmark of successful individuals. Remembering names, dates, and key details strengthens relationships, builds trust, and enhances productivity. It signals attentiveness and empathy, making others feel valued. With the rise of technology, memory is becoming less relied upon, and an overdependence on digital tools can weaken cognitive abilities. Like a muscle, memory must be exercised to remain strong. Those who naturally possess a sharp memory should hone it rather than let it atrophy.

### *Intelligence*

---

*"Wise men learn from the mistakes of others, mediocre men from their own, but fools never learn."*

---

Intelligence, often linked to memory, is more than just knowledge; it is the ability to make sound decisions, exercise discernment, and control emotions. Intelligent individuals know what to say, when to say it, and how to act appropriately in any given situation.

Some are naturally quick-witted, their minds forming connections faster than others. However, intelligence, like any gift, must be nurtured. Knowledge is only valuable when applied effectively, and true wisdom lies in learning from both personal experiences and the experiences of others.

### *Charisma*

Charisma is an elusive yet powerful quality.[5] Charismatic individuals draw people in effortlessly, making others feel comfortable and valued. They possess keen emotional intelligence, a well-developed sense of humor, and an innate ability to uplift and influence those around them.

However, charisma can be misused. Some squander it on shallow entertainment, and others wield it manipulatively for personal gain. To be a force for good, charisma must be coupled with integrity and self-awareness.

### *Brilliance*

Brilliance is the ability to think quickly, read between the lines, and respond effectively to unexpected situations. It is a sharpness of mind that allows individuals to turn challenges into opportunities. One of the greatest examples of wit and brilliance comes from Winston Churchill. He was famous for his sharp tongue and quick comebacks. Lady Astor, a political rival, once told him, "Winston, if you were my husband, I'd poison your tea."

---

[5]Antonakis, J., Fenley, M., & Liechti, S. (2012). Learning charisma: Transform yourself into the person others want to follow. *Harvard Business Review, 90*(6), 127–130.

Without missing a beat, Churchill replied, "Madam, if you were my wife, I'd drink it."

This kind of quick-witted humor—sharp, unexpected, and perfectly timed—is a hallmark of brilliance.

### *Courage*

Courage is not the absence of fear but the determination to act despite it. Many people imagine courage to be an inborn personality trait, something you either have or you don't. In reality, courage is a practiced habit, strengthened each time we choose to move forward even when we feel uncertain or afraid.

This is an important distinction for this chapter. Some qualities we discuss, such as temperament or natural talent, may be partly innate. But the traits that shape lasting success—including courage, discipline, resilience, and perseverance—are learned and developed over time. Successful individuals are not simply born different; they become different by repeatedly making bold decisions, taking risks, and enduring adversity until these behaviors become part of who they are.

## Two Ways People React to Their Natural Talents

People tend to react to their natural talents in one of two ways:

### *1. Resentment and Comparison*

Many lament the gifts they lack, focusing on their perceived deficiencies rather than their strengths. They feel shortchanged by life, using negative talk like, *"If only I were taller, funnier, braver, or smarter."* This mindset fosters envy and complacency, preventing success before the journey even begins.

### 2. Gratitude and Stewardship

Other people choose to be grateful, embracing their gifts—however modest—and maximizing them. They see their talents as divine blessings and take responsibility for developing them. Even those with significant obstacles can achieve greatness when they focus on what they *can* do rather than what they *cannot*.

Making the most of our natural talents is the cornerstone of a successful life. Our abilities are gifts from God, and what we do with them is our gift back to Him and to those around us. By recognizing and cultivating our unique strengths, we lay the foundation for a life of purpose, impact, and fulfillment.

## Opportunities and Experiences

The second category of natural attributes includes the opportunities and experiences that shape our lives. While our DNA is a gift from God, the opportunities and experiences we encounter—many of which are beyond our control—also play a crucial role. We can influence some of them, but most are external factors. What we can control, however, is our response to them. Below are several key opportunities and experiences that influence success, though many others exist.

### 1. Family

A person's family can significantly impact their success or failure. None of us chooses the family into which we are born. During childhood, we have little ability to influence family dynamics. Some people grow up in loving, secure homes that provide a strong foundation, while others experience neglect, tension, abandonment, or even abuse. Family shapes our first habits, thought patterns, and perception of what is "normal."

A strong family foundation can also provide financial advantages. In entrepreneurship, it is often said that startups rely on funding from family, friends, and fools. In the United States, wealth inheritance also plays a significant role in financial success. Studies suggest that a substantial portion of high-net-worth individuals—particularly those with assets exceeding $5 million—have inherited at least part of their wealth from previous generations. While the American Dream emphasizes self-made success, the reality is that generational wealth remains a key factor in financial mobility.[6] The transfer of wealth through family estates, business ownership, and trust funds continues to shape economic opportunities, with factors like tax policies and investment strategies influencing wealth retention and growth.

On the other hand, family can also be a source of tension and frustration. Many people hold unspoken expectations of their families, leading to disappointment. Successful individuals learn to manage their expectations rather than trying to control their families. I have met financially and socially successful families whose children or grandchildren squandered their inheritance due to greed or a need to prove independence. Managing success is just as important as achieving it.

### *2. Education*

Education—whether formal, informal, guided by a mentor, or acquired through life experiences—is a vital factor in success. Yet access to education often depends on circumstances beyond our control.

As a child, I struggled with concentration due to my high energy levels. One spring, between third and fourth grade, my mother devised an ingenious solution. Coloring books were expensive, and our family had limited resources. Instead, she bought semi-

[6] Roeloffs, M. (2023, November 30). New billionaires inherited more than they earned last year, UBS report says. *Forbes*. https://www.forbes.com/sites/maryroeloffs/2023/11/30/new-billionaires-inherited-more-than-they-earned-last-year-ubs-report-says/.

transparent paper and had me trace the outlines of coloring book images so we could color them repeatedly in different shades. This simple exercise taught me focus and discipline, skills that later helped me write multiple articles and books such as the one you are reading.

### *3. Travel*

Exposure to different cultures through travel is another powerful opportunity. Creativity—an essential element of success—is nurtured through both reading and travel. When we leave our comfort level, we face new and unexpected situations, try unfamiliar foods, and expand our perspectives.

Some people travel for leisure, while others move abroad in search of work or refuge from war or disaster. One reason I am optimistic about America's future is the growing number of Americans who have broadened their horizons through international travel and cross-cultural experiences. While travel alone does not guarantee success, history shows that individuals and nations benefit from exposure to the world. Countries like Israel and Ireland have thrived due, in part, to the experiences of their diasporas.

### *4. Foreign Languages*

Fluency in multiple languages is a common trait among successful individuals.[7] While formal language courses are valuable, they can sometimes result in years of study without true fluency. The goal of learning a foreign language should be natural interaction with native speakers, not just earning a certificate. In our interconnected world, language skills open doors. The United States, as a global economic and cultural powerhouse, benefits from linguistic

---

[7] Welch, D., Welch, L., & Piekkari, R. (2005). Speaking in tongues: The importance of language in international management processes. *International Studies of Management & Organization, 35*(1), 10–27.

diversity due to its immigrant population and international business ties. While one can achieve success speaking only English, being monolingual can be a limitation in an increasingly interconnected world. Research suggests that multilingualism enhances cognitive function, creativity, and career opportunities.[8]

Master the English language in reading, writing, and conversation. Additionally, Spanish is highly valuable within the U.S. and Latin America, while Mandarin Chinese offers a strategic advantage in the global economy. French and German can also be beneficial for those engaging with European markets and international diplomacy.

### *5. Lack of Favorable Circumstances*

Many successful people rise to leadership because there was no one else to step up. Perhaps no one wanted to lead a class, take on a new project, or assume responsibility for a struggling department. Many entrepreneurs build businesses after losing jobs simply because they had no other option.

One of my clients runs a successful building maintenance company. He originally worked as a translator for a German firm in Romania that eventually withdrew from the country. The company still had contracts to fulfill, and no one was willing to take over the business. With no one else stepping up, he took the risk. Today, he manages hundreds of employees and leads a company with millions in revenue, all because he seized an opportunity others overlooked.

### *6. Traumatic Events*

Life-altering events such as illnesses, accidents, relocations, and losses can be pivotal. Most people go through life without deep

---

[8] Fürst, G., & Grin, F. (2023). Multilingualism, multicultural experience, cognition, and creativity. *Frontiers in Psychology, 14,* 1155158. https://doi.org/10.3389/fpsyg.2023.1155158.

reflection, avoiding existential questions like: *Who am I? Why am I alive? What is my purpose? What happens after death?* The modern world offers endless distractions to keep us from contemplating such matters. However, trauma forces us to re-evaluate our lives.

Most successful people I have met have faced significant hardships,[9] such as

- Entrepreneurs who started businesses after losing their job
- Academics who mastered new subjects while recovering in hospital beds
- Politicians who positively changed after major defeats
- Artists who thrived despite disabilities
- Leaders who changed the world following assassination attempts or profound spiritual experiences

However, not all people who endure trauma find success. Many remain trapped in cycles of self-pity, passing on suffering to others. *I was betrayed, so I betray others. I was cheated, so I cheat in return.* This mindset perpetuates misery. Successful individuals break this cycle. They are not overcome by evil; instead, they overcome evil with good.

Consider how pearls are made. When an irritant, such as a grain of sand or a parasite, enters an oyster or mussel, it causes discomfort and irritation. The soft tissue inside the shell reacts to the intruder by secreting a substance called *nacre* (also known as mother-of-pearl). This substance is made up of layers of minerals and proteins that coat the irritant to protect the oyster from further harm.

---

[9] Drucker, P. F. (2004). What makes an effective executive. *Harvard Business Review, 82*(6), 58–63.

Just as the oyster turns pain into beauty, we can use life's challenges and hardships to build resilience, wisdom, and personal growth. The pain may be an unavoidable part of life, but how we respond to it—just like the oyster—determines what we become. A traumatic event does not define success or failure; our response to it does.

## Pride: The Temptation of the Gifted

We are all born with natural endowments—talents, opportunities, and experiences—that shape who we are. However, there is a particular danger for those who possess these gifts, including those who learn how to maximize them, that can lead to their downfall: pride.

Gifted individuals, especially those who have survived trauma, often face the temptation of becoming proud and arrogant. As the saying goes, "High mountains have deep valleys." While success can be a reward for overcoming challenges, it can also make us vulnerable to pride. Pride arises when we become self-sufficient, believing we no longer need anyone, that we have all the answers, and that we can overcome even the worst obstacles alone. This mindset turns our gifts into a reason to boast. We risk becoming someone who always has something to say, constantly offering opinions but never taking responsibility for their actions or admitting their mistakes. It's the person who dominates conversations, always wanting to be heard and validated yet rarely reflecting on their own shortcomings. They may appear confident or even arrogant, but their inability to acknowledge their errors can make them seem disconnected or even insincere to those around them. Instead of fostering meaningful relationships, this behavior can create alienation as people begin to feel that their opinions are undervalued and that the individual is more concerned with being right than with building genuine connections.

This kind of pride can breed contempt for others, especially those who may not share our achievements. Successful individuals sometimes begin to see the world in black and white, viewing others as "poor" or "helpless." The underlying message is, "If I made it, why can't you?" This attitude often strains relationships with loved ones—children, employees, and students. The arrogance of pride can alienate those we care about and wish to help, damaging the very connections that might have made us truly successful in the first place.

Pride is the devil's original sin against God. As C. S. Lewis wisely observed, "Pride leads to all other vices; it is the complete anti-God state of mind."[10] Though we know the dangers of pride, many successful individuals still fall prey to it. There are three key factors that fuel pride, which we must be aware of and actively counteract.

- **Objective and quantifiable results** – High sales, accolades, social media followers, or public recognition can create a sense of superiority. These results can be important, but the danger lies in taking too much credit for them and forgetting the contributions of others.
- **Praise and admiration from others** – There is nothing wrong with accepting compliments or recognition, but when we base our value on the opinions of others, we risk losing our sense of self-

[10] Lewis, C. S. (2001). *Mere Christianity*. HarperOne. (Original work published 1952).

worth. Sadly, many people overspend and chase status to impress people they don't even truly care about.

- **Comparison to others** – Some successful individuals surround themselves with less competent people to feel superior. They may even resent anyone who challenges or compares themselves to the "successful" person. This creates a toxic environment where people use and manipulate the gifted person for their own gain.

*Why is pride so dangerous?*

- **It alienates others.** I have seen gifted people who were so consumed by their pride that they lost everyone who once supported them. They became unbearable, and eventually, even their partners, employees, and friends walked away. Pride isolates us.
- **Pride prevents us from seizing new opportunities.** Some people would rather remain at the top of their current situation, no matter how limited, than risk failing at something new. But avoiding new challenges, even at the risk of embarrassment, can prevent us from growing further.
- **Pride gives us a false sense of security.[11]** Yesterday's successes don't guarantee tomorrow's. Many organizations, countries, and individuals have been undone by resting on the laurels of past achievements. Just because I was successful once

[11] Keltner, D. (2016). Don't let power corrupt you. *Harvard Business Review, 94*(10), 112-115.

> does not ensure future success. It is dangerous to assume that past glory will carry us forward.

When we fall into the trap of pride, we forget the reality that we are all created beings, blessed with talents and placed in a larger ecosystem that supports us. Our pride turns humility into contempt and good humor into bad jokes. Instead of building relationships, we tear them down. As the saying goes, "Pride goes before destruction, a haughty spirit before a fall" (Prov. 16:18).

I have witnessed this in people who have worked abroad and returned to their home country. Though not particularly wealthy, some feel compelled to flaunt their success in front of others, wearing flashy clothes, driving expensive cars, or borrowing money just to prove how well they are doing. This behavior ultimately alienates others and reflects the emptiness of pride.

In the end, pride is the temptation of the gifted, a temptation that can turn success into failure and relationships into ruins. The antidote is humility, the recognition that our gifts are not ours alone but are meant to be shared with others.

## Herculean Spikes

As we reach the conclusion of this chapter, I have both good news and not-so-good news. The good news is that pride can be curbed and channeled. The not-so-good news is that the temptation of pride is something we must contend with throughout our lives. We can never fully eliminate it, only control it.

To explain how to master pride, let's consider the myth of Hercules and the Twelve Labors. Hercules, one of the strongest figures in Greek mythology, was ordered to perform 12 seemingly impossible tasks as punishment for a past crime. These labors ranged from slaying the Nemean Lion to capturing the Golden Hind of Artemis. Hercules was, of course, a figure of immense strength, but his journey was marked by both physical and moral challenges.

During these labors, Hercules had to confront not only the external monsters and challenges but also his own weaknesses: pride, arrogance, and self-doubt. The metaphorical "spikes" that helped Hercules stay grounded in the face of these tasks were the self-awareness and humility required to complete each one. For example, when he captured the Erymanthian Boar, Hercules didn't rely on sheer strength alone; he also had to show patience and strategy. When facing the Stymphalian Birds, he had to adapt, using not just his might but his ingenuity to succeed.

Like Hercules, when we are confronted by pride, we must adopt metaphorical "spikes" to keep us grounded. For Hercules, these were the virtues of strategy, humility, adaptability, and resilience—each of which kept him from being consumed by his own pride in his power.

To explain how to master pride, let's also consider the story of Thomas Edison, one of the greatest inventors in history, who faced many challenges on his journey to invent the light bulb. In his early years, Edison's experiments were not successful. His first attempts to create a working light bulb failed repeatedly. He had to test thousands of different filaments and designs, often in complete isolation, enduring long hours of trial and error.

The discomfort Edison experienced was not just physical but also psychological. The relentless failures wore him down, and many people around him doubted his ability to ever achieve success. Yet Edison believed that failure was just another step toward finding the right solution. He famously said, "I have not failed. I've just found 10,000 ways that won't work." In this process, Edison imposed several Herculean "spikes" upon himself that pushed him past his limits.

- **Endurance in Isolation** – Edison often worked long hours, sometimes going days without sleep. He was willing to sacrifice comfort, social interactions, and basic needs like sleep because he believed in the bigger goal of changing the world with his invention.

- **Mental Resilience** – Edison deliberately confronted the frustration of failure, knowing that each failure was a valuable lesson. Rather than wallowing in despair, he used each setback as a necessary discomfort that brought him closer to success.
- **Physical Discomfort** – In some cases, Edison's experiments were dangerous, and he worked in environments that were often hot, messy, and hazardous. He did not shy away from physical discomfort, understanding that it was a small price to pay for eventual success.
- **Self-Criticism and Relentless Iteration** – Edison didn't allow himself to be satisfied with half-baked solutions. Even when he found a working filament, he continued testing, refining, and improving it. This self-imposed Herculean "spike" of constantly evaluating and criticizing his own work ensured that he didn't settle for mediocrity.

Through his self-imposed discomforts, Edison eventually succeeded. In 1879, he developed a practical, long-lasting light bulb. His relentless pursuit of success, fueled by his ability to make himself uncomfortable, revolutionized the world and paved the way for countless innovations.

The story of Edison demonstrates how great success often requires us to face uncomfortable truths about our limitations, endure physical and emotional strain, and impose self-discipline. These "spikes" are essential for personal and professional growth, just as Edison's self-imposed discomforts were essential to his success in inventing the light bulb.

In the same way, there are four "spikes" we can use to master pride. These spikes act as reminders that pride can be managed through constant reflection and humility. No matter how powerful or capable we feel, the journey of mastering pride involves not just the use of our strengths but the cultivation of wisdom, humility, and perseverance. Here's how we can do it.

## Spike 1 – Realize you are a steward, not an owner.

The first "spike" is recognizing that we are stewards rather than owners. Everything we have, whether good or bad, is a gift. We will carry nothing with us when we leave this world. Alexander the Great, for example, instructed that his hands be left exposed in his grave to show that he couldn't take his wealth with him. When we see ourselves as owners, we become possessive, seeing others only in terms of what they can offer us. This narrow perspective leads to dissatisfaction, stress, and even despair when things go wrong. In contrast, stewards take care of what's entrusted to them with a healthy detachment. They work hard, stay consistent, and remain optimistic, even in tough times, knowing that Someone greater is in control. When faced with failure, such as bankruptcy, a steward sees it as a learning opportunity, while an owner might see it as the end.

## Spike 2 – Practice discreet altruism.

The second "spike" is discreet altruism—that is, using our gifts, opportunities, and resources to help others without seeking recognition. In today's social-media-driven world, it's tempting to flaunt our successes and generosity, but these only feed our pride. Discreet altruism is the antidote. We offer our help without broadcasting it. This practice aligns with Christian teaching, as it demonstrates faith in God's rewards rather than the praise of men. It's a powerful way to resist the urge to seek validation and to remind ourselves that our worth is not tied to public approval.

## Spike 3 - Recognize the final balance sheet.

The third "spike" is the awareness of the final balance sheet and our inevitable mortality. Benjamin Franklin famously said, "The only certainties in life are death and taxes." In the same spirit, I ask my students at Emanuel University of Oradea to start their life plan by writing their own obituary. This exercise forces us to confront the reality of death and consider how we will be remembered. Christian teaching holds that salvation is a gift, and nothing we do can change our fate after death. When we reflect on this existential reality, any pride over earthly accomplishments shrinks in comparison. Life's true balance isn't found in material success but in how we've lived and loved.

## Spike 4 - Understand that character matters more than achievements.

---

*Some of the most influential people in history were known not for their wealth but for their* ***humility*** *and* ***integrity****.*

---

The fourth "spike" is realizing that character is more important than material achievements. It's easy to become enamored with what we can acquire, and pride often follows material success. The antidote to this is refocusing on our character. Material goods are fleeting, but our character and relationships define us. Some of the most influential people in history were known not for their wealth or status but for their humility and integrity. They did not see themselves as superior but understood that their true value lay in their character. They built their lives around core values and faith, which guided them through their successes without losing sight of what truly mattered.

By embracing these four "spikes," we can keep pride in check, ensuring that our successes don't lead us down a path of arrogance and alienation. Instead, we'll cultivate humility, strengthen our relationships, and stay grounded in what truly matters.

## Reflection and Discussion

1. *Where do I see this strength—and its shadow—in my own life?*

2. *What situations most often trigger the temptation connected to this strength?*

3. *What safeguards or disciplines can I put in place to cultivate the strength while resisting its temptation?*

4. *Who in my life models this strength well, and what can I learn from their example?*

## Further Reading

Brand, P., & Yancey, P. (2014). *A disease so strange: A novel*. Tyndale House Publishers.

Currey, M. (2013). *Daily rituals: How artists work*. Knopf.

Dalio, R. (2017). *Principles: Life and work*. Simon & Schuster.

David, D. (2017). *The psychology of the Roman people: Psychological profiling of the Romans in a cognitive-experimental monograph*. Cambridge Scholars Publishing.

Dias, D. (2021). *The ten human typologies: Who we are and who we could be*. Routledge.

Gladwell, M. (2000). *The tipping point: How little things can make a big difference*. Little, Brown.

Marshall, T. (2021). *The power of geography: Ten maps that reveal the future of the world*. Elliott & Thompson.

Maxwell, J. C. (1993). *Developing the leader within you*. Thomas Nelson.

Packer, J. I. (1973). *Knowing God*. InterVarsity Press.

Taleb, N. N. (2007). *The black swan: The impact of the highly improbable*. Random House.

Tracy, B., & Stein, C. T. (2001). *Kiss that frog! 12 great ways to turn negatives into positives in your life and work*. Berrett-Koehler Publishers.

Ziglar, Z. (2000). *The psychology of selling*. Thomas Nelson.

---

*Both sons have an alcoholic father.*
*One son also becomes an alcoholic.*
*The other becomes a successful businessman.*
*When they are both asked why they became the way they did, they both reply, "Because my father was an alcoholic."*

---

# 2

# PERSUASIVENESS VS. DISHONESTY

A PUBLISHING HOUSE ONCE HIRED A SALESMAN WITH a stutter. To everyone's surprise, he outsold his colleagues. When asked about his technique, he replied, "I knock on the door and ask if they want to buy an encyclopedia, or should I read them the first chapter?"

The second key trait I have observed in successful people is their ability to negotiate, sell, and persuade others of their values and ideas. While I don't entirely agree with the statement, "You don't get what you deserve; you get what you bargain for," I do believe there's a kernel of truth to it. From my observations, successful individuals don't passively accept life as it is. Instead, they take proactive steps to improve their situations. I firmly believe that only 5 percent of life is shaped by circumstances, while 95 percent is shaped by how we respond to those circumstances.

I've encountered talented individuals with great prospects, wealthy families, and impressive opportunities who missed out on success due to poor decisions. On the other hand, I've met people with limited resources who thrived because they chose to react positively and work hard, making the most of what they had. When life handed them lemons, they made lemonade.

Phrases like "it should be" or "it would be nice if" often reflect idealistic thinking that can be dangerous. These expressions highlight what we *wish* or *hope* for, but they tend to create unrealistic expectations. For example, many people may say, "People should be treated fairly" or "Leaders should act with integrity." While these ideals are important, focusing too much on "what should be" without acting on or recognizing the reality of the situation can lead to frustration and inaction. Instead of passively waiting for things to improve, successful individuals take charge, negotiate, and work toward creating the change they desire. For example, people say, "Intellectuals should be appreciated for their worth" or "Honest and hardworking people should be promoted to leadership positions." While I agree these things *should* happen, idealized expectations often lead to disappointment. Solomon wisely noted, "Hope deferred makes the heart sick" (Prov. 13:12). I've encountered many who are disillusioned because they passively wait for the world to change on its own.

In contrast, successful people understand that nothing in life happens without persuasion and negotiation. Change requires proactive action, whether it's improving a situation, creating new opportunities, or negotiating terms.

Consider someone looking to buy a house priced at $300,000, committing to 30 years of mortgage payments. What if they could negotiate the price down to $250,000? Or imagine someone interviewing for a job offering $50,000 per year. What difference would negotiating a salary of $60,000 make? Negotiation may be a short-term event that lasts a few hours or days, but the long-term impact it can have on someone's financial stability and overall life is significant. The power of a successful negotiation can improve not just the immediate situation but also set the stage for long-term success. Successful people embrace the importance of persuasiveness and selling. They recognize its power and do their best to hone their negotiating skills. They know how to maximize opportunities through natural gifts, preparation, and experience.

---

*Negotiation is a short-term event that can have a long-term impact.*

---

In the first part of this chapter, we'll explore seven essential traits of a good negotiator:

1. Pragmatism
2. Preparation
3. Communication
4. Appearance
5. Attention to others' preferences
6. Charisma
7. Resilience or emotional mastery

The great news is that anyone can become a better negotiator or salesperson! However, as with any skill, there are temptations to guard against. In the case of persuasiveness, the temptation is dishonesty. We will discuss what lying looks like in negotiations, the justifications people use for dishonesty, and its repercussions on our lives. Finally, we'll conclude with some strategies to prevent dishonesty because a key to success is being a persuasive negotiator without sacrificing your integrity or credibility.

## What Makes a Good Negotiator?

### *1. Pragmatism*

A strong negotiator embraces constructive pragmatism,[12] a mindset that balances realism with optimism. In contrast to an idealistic projection, I define pragmatism as a realistic perspective. Pragmatism is a clear and true understanding of reality, without the loss of joy and optimism. Pragmatism is the opposite of idealism. In the idealistic paradigm, we resignedly discuss how things should be. In constructive pragmatism, we accept reality as it is and discuss what we can

[12] Malhotra, D., & Bazerman, M. (2007). *Negotiation genius: How to overcome obstacles and achieve brilliant results at the bargaining table and beyond*. Bantam.

do to improve it. Unlike idealists who dwell on how things *should* be, pragmatic negotiators accept reality as it is and focus on what can be improved. The constructive pragmatist starts from the fundamental notion that, with the help of God and those around him, he can negotiate an improvement in the situation. He believes that, despite a negative past or the current reality, the future can be better and that he can do something to improve it.

For example, an idealist might lament that their parents can't afford to buy them a house. A pragmatist, on the other hand, acknowledges her family's financial limits and acts, perhaps enrolling in a digital marketing course to increase her earning potential.

Constructive pragmatism is crucial because it prevents cynicism, discouragement, and laziness. A pragmatic negotiator believes that—with effort, faith, and the right support system—they can create a better future. Here are two ways to cultivate this mindset.

*Guard your mind.*

What you consume shapes your thinking. Do you focus on negativity, or do you seek out success stories and role models? Ask yourself the following questions:

- Do I feed myself with negative news and harmful examples, or do I nourish my mind with success stories?
- Do I read about or watch people who have succeeded in life or those who wallow in misery?

*Surround yourself with positive role models.*

The people around you influence your mindset. Connect with those who uplift and inspire you. Even though it's not easy and requires effort, cultivate friendships with people who build you up. Use technology and communication to connect with people who are great role models and who can support you on your journey toward success. In the short term, you may feel better around cynics and mockers; however, in the long run, such people will prevent your growth. Bad company corrupts good habits.

### 2. Preparation

Success is where opportunity meets preparation. Yet many people wait for opportunities without preparing for them. A shocking number of people walk into interviews, important meetings, or negotiations without doing their homework.

---

*Success is where opportunity meets preparation.*

---

Preparation is pre-thinking, visualizing scenarios, crafting responses, and anticipating objections. Strong negotiators prepare thoroughly, giving them confidence and control. Good negotiators not only prepare presentation materials but also anticipate the inevitable objections from their counterparts. The more prepared you are for a negotiation, the more confident you will be. The more prepared you are for a sale, the better you will be at controlling your emotions and not being shocked by an objection or rejection. Preparation involves the ability to see the situation from the other person's perspective and to speak or present in terms that resonate with them. Technology makes it easier than ever to research people and institutions before entering negotiations. Arrogance in assuming you can "wing it" is a mistake.

### 3. Communication

Most people assume great negotiators are naturally persuasive speakers. While communication is key, it's a learned skill rather than an innate talent. Typically, when we think of a good negotiator or a "born" salesperson, we think of their ability to communicate. They seem to have no shame or inhibitions, saying what the rest of us only think. It's as if they always have the right words for the right situation and an extraordinary sense of timing. Through communication, they know how to assert their ideas and will, and most of the time, those around them listen and follow. Introverts prefer to communicate in writing and have the advantage of having their ideas and words remain, but the most impactful and influential communicators know how to both write and speak.

Abraham Lincoln was a master of written communication, carefully crafting letters and documents that shaped the nation's course. Lincoln's combination of eloquent speeches and powerful written works helped him navigate the Civil War, influence public opinion, and ultimately shape the future of the United States.

Effective communicators can articulate their thoughts clearly, whether in writing or speech. To improve communication skills:

- **Be intentional** – Avoid careless, unfocused speech.
- **Record yourself** – Listening to or watching yourself can reveal areas for improvement.
- **Expand your vocabulary** – Learn new words to enhance clarity and precision.

### *4. Attractiveness*

Over 70 percent of communication is non-verbal,[13] and first impressions matter. We don't get a second chance to make a first impression. Of course, there are exceptions to this rule, but we are emotional beings, and many decisions are made sentimentally or unconsciously. Attractiveness could also be categorized as a natural gift, but successful people know how to become attractive with the qualities they have—not with those they wish they had. They focus on what they have, not on what they lack. A negotiator's appearance and demeanor influence how others perceive them. Here are some key aspects of attractiveness:

---

[13] Mehrabian, A. (2017). *Nonverbal communication*. Routledge.

- **Hygiene and grooming** – Basics like brushing your teeth, combing your hair, and using deodorant make a difference.
- **Wardrobe** – Your clothing sends a message. A well-dressed person exudes confidence, while a sloppy appearance can signal insecurity.
- **Facial expressions and attitude** – A deadpan or arrogant demeanor can overshadow even the best negotiation skills. Smiling and treating others with respect increases likability and effectiveness.

When we improve our appearance and take care of ourselves, our self-esteem, productivity, and reputation will also grow.

---

*We don't get a second chance to make a first impression.*

---

### *5. Emotional Intelligence*

A great negotiator understands people—not just numbers. Successful negotiators don't seek victory at any cost; they aim for win-win scenarios that foster long-term relationships. Emotional intelligence (EQ) or social intelligence[14] allows you to read between the lines, anticipate reactions, and tailor your approach.

How can we develop our emotional intelligence? A starting point is empathy or altruism. It is the fulfillment of the Golden Rule, "Do unto others as you would have them do unto you." Try to understand the situation from the other person's perspective. Empathize with that person and try to offer solutions to the problems they are facing. Do your homework regarding the person or institution with whom you are negotiating. Study similar situations or people

[14] Goleman, D. (1995). *Emotional intelligence: Why it can matter more than IQ*. Bantam Books.

to know what the optimal approach is. Learn to read between the lines and understand the unspoken things.

Sometimes the buyer doesn't know what they want or is unaware of the importance of certain things. I remember a newly married couple who wanted to buy furniture for their bedroom with a budget of only $1,000. Their disappointment was great when they realized they could only buy part of the furniture with that amount of money. Such clients need help understanding reality.

To further enhance EQ:

- **Develop empathy** – Understand the other person's perspective and motivations.
- **Do your homework** – Learn about the people you're negotiating with. What matters to them? What are their challenges?
- **Observe non-verbal cues** – Sometimes what's left unsaid is more important than spoken words.

### *6. Charisma and Humor*

Charisma is the ability to create an engaging atmosphere, knowing the right joke for the right moment and making people feel at ease. Many skilled negotiators use humor to defuse tension, win people over, and navigate difficult situations.

A prime example is President Ronald Reagan. During the 1984 presidential campaign, concerns about his age were mounting. When asked if he had the stamina for another term, Reagan quipped, "I will not make age an issue of this campaign. I am not going to exploit, for political purposes, my opponent's youth and inexperience." Even his opponent, Walter Mondale, couldn't help but laugh. Reagan's humor not only defused a tough moment but also reinforced his confidence and likability, key traits of a charismatic leader. Humor isn't just entertainment; it's a tool that fosters connection and resilience.

Everyone is born with charisma, even though this may not be obvious because many have suppressed it for various reasons. The good news is that anyone can improve their charisma and cultivate their sense of humor. A great book on this subject is *How to Win Friends and Influence People*. The recommendations Carnegie offers for improving your charisma include tips such as don't complain, don't criticize, and don't gossip.

Have a good filter for the things you store in your mind and heart and make a conscious effort to feed yourself with positive things. When speaking with someone, take a genuine interest in their situation and well-being. Encourage people to talk about the topics that matter most to them and see the world from their perspective.

### *7. Resilience and Emotional Control*

Skilled negotiators are mentally tough. They don't crumble under rejection or setbacks. Instead, they view challenges as part of the process. I define resilience as the ability to overcome rejection, defeat, disappointment, or betrayal. Feelings are the mental software that determines our functioning as social beings. One of the problems I observe, especially among young people, is the mistaken expectation that life should be free of rejections or disappointments. Some feed on an idealized version of life, one without problems, rejections, lies, cruelty, opposition, betrayal, or disappointment. A good negotiator possesses impressive mental tenacity.[15] They know how to manage their emotions well. They don't get overly excited in positive situations, nor do they get overly discouraged in negative ones. However, the most important thing is that when (not *if*) they face defeats, they know how to bounce back. True failure is not when you fail but when you stop trying to start over.

---

[15] Seligman, M. E. P. (2011). Building resilience. *Harvard Business Review*, 89(4), 100–102.

How can you develop your resilience and control your feelings more effectively? As with other skills, it's a matter of practice. The more you do it, the more accustomed you will become. To build resilience,

- **Keep moving forward** – It comes down to willpower. When you face rejection, even if it affects you emotionally, pick up the phone and try again. Be prepared for any situation, including backup options in case of rejection. Don't start feeling sorry for yourself, even if you have reasons to, and don't let your imagination take you into the realm of fantasy.
- **Manage expectations** – Unrealistic hopes lead to disappointment. The more grandiose and idealized your expectations, the greater the chances of disappointment.
- **Learn from mistakes** – If something isn't working, change your approach. The best way to recover from disappointment is to avoid it. I've met many people who make the same mistakes in similar situations and are surprised when they get the same results, ignoring the warning that insanity is doing the same thing repeatedly and expecting different results.
- **Realize true failure isn't falling** – Instead, true failure is refusing to get back up.

In this section, I've outlined some traits of people skilled at negotiations and sales. First, they demonstrate constructive pragmatism that helps them see the world as it is, not as they would like it to be. Second, they understand the importance of preparation. Third is the ability to communicate both verbally and in writing. The fourth component is attractiveness and how they present themselves. The fifth element is attention to the preferences and personalities of others, and the sixth is charisma and a sense of humor. Finally, persuasive negotiators and salespeople know how to control their emotions with the help of willpower.

Regardless of natural abilities, anyone can develop these skills with effort and intention. Persuasiveness opens doors, improves opportunities, and leads to long-term success. However, persuasiveness also comes with the temptation to deceive. In the next section, we will explore the risks of deception and how to avoid them.

## Dishonesty: The Temptation of a Persuasive Negotiator

When I returned to Romania in 1995, I had the privilege of working with an entrepreneur from Arad, Romania, who later became a friend and client. He shared the story of how he started his business. Together with a more charismatic and intelligent associate, he participated in the privatization of a plastics factory. As outsiders to the communist system, they faced numerous setbacks and disappointments. However, through hard work, patience, creativity, and faith, they built a company with an annual turnover exceeding one million Deutschmarks. Yet his partner had a fatal flaw: dishonesty.

At first, it seemed harmless—a small lie here and there. But over time, deception became his way of life. He embezzled money, created a fraudulent shell company, borrowed from loan sharks, and eventually spiraled into addiction. His personal life unraveled. He abandoned his wife and children, turned to drugs and alcohol, and ultimately became a broken man. Through tears, my friend recounted the deep personal and professional pain caused by his partner's deception. This story illustrates a crucial truth: lying is not just a harmless tool in negotiation or business; it can destroy lives.

In this section, I will explore what lying is, the justifications we create for it, and its profound repercussions. Whether we are natural-born salespeople or not, we all face the temptation to lie and must be aware of its dangers.

## What Is Lying?

Most people are quick to recognize lies in others but struggle to acknowledge their own. A lie is any untruthful thought, word, or action. Often, it starts unconsciously; we say something without verifying its truth. Many justify dishonesty by claiming they are being polite or sparing someone's feelings. Others deceive to gain an advantage, hoping the truth will never come to light.

Some companies even build their business models around customer ignorance, banking on people not knowing the truth or lacking alternatives. When their deception is exposed, they justify it, offer excuses, and claim it was necessary. A book I recommend on this subject is *The Honest Truth About Dishonesty: How We Lie to Everyone—Especially Ourselves.*[16] Even if we think that lying is justified or has no repercussions on our character and reputation, in reality, lying is devastating.

Lying starts with self-deception. We easily recognize dishonesty in others, yet we justify our own, convincing ourselves that it's harmless or even necessary. We make promises we can't keep, excuse our actions by blaming stress or a hectic schedule, and tell ourselves that a little dishonesty won't hurt. There's an old saying that reflects this mindset: "The end justifies the means." It's the idea that bending the truth is acceptable as long as it helps us get where we want to go. As the saying goes, "A little white lie never hurt anyone." This phrase reflects the common belief that certain lies are harmless or even beneficial, especially when told to avoid conflict or spare someone's feelings. However, it also highlights the slippery slope of rationalizing dishonesty.

But small lies accumulate. They become habits. Some people lie so often that they deceive even when there is no need. At first, lying seems to bring short-term benefits: money, influence, and

---

[16] Ariely, D., & Jones, S. (2012). *The honest truth about dishonesty: How we lie to everyone—especially ourselves.* HarperCollins.

opportunities. In the long run, it erodes integrity, damages relationships, and leads to ruin.

## How Do We Justify Lying?

Despite knowing the dangers of dishonesty, we build elaborate justifications for it.

### *1. Redefining the Truth*

Some claim truth is subjective. They see deception clearly in others but rationalize it in themselves. Years ago, while working with Transparency International Romania, I helped organize an "Integrity for Prosperity" campaign across 15 cities. One of our biggest discoveries? Many people lacked a clear definition of corruption or dishonesty. If we cannot define lying, how can we avoid it?

### *2. "Everyone Does It"*

At business conferences, I sometimes hear, "Professor, everyone does it. We don't have a choice."

My response? "For centuries, millions of so-called 'civilized' people practiced slavery in Europe and America. That didn't make it moral or justified." Just because something is common doesn't make it right.

### *3. Believing the Lie Will Never Be Discovered*

People assume that if no one finds out, no harm is done. But even if others remain unaware, the liar knows. Guilt erodes motivation, enthusiasm, and effectiveness. As Murphy's Law suggests, if something can go wrong, it likely will, and at the worst possible moment.

### *4. Abusing God's Grace*

Some justify a life of dishonesty by claiming that God forgives all sins. While it is true that God forgives, using His mercy as an excuse to continue lying reveals a misunderstanding of both His grace and the patience of those around us.

At its core, lying is linked to selfishness. People prioritize their desires over integrity, believing others must forgive them no matter what. Some even manipulate religious teachings, demanding submission from their families while using deception to control them. But true submission and helpfulness do not mean enabling dishonesty.

## The Consequences of Lying

Lying always has consequences, whether we acknowledge them or not. There is a cosmic law that balances the accounts and rewards each person according to their deeds.

### *1. Internal Confusion and Self-Doubt*

A habitual liar must constantly remember past deceptions, leading to anxiety and insecurity.

### *2. Stunted Personal Growth*

Those who live in deception avoid confronting their weaknesses. Rather than improving, they spend their energy justifying their mistakes.

### *3. Loss of Trust and Reputation*

Trust is difficult to build but easy to destroy. I have seen the painful consequences of broken trust: children unwilling to follow their parents' footsteps, employees distrusting their leaders, customers abandoning dishonest businesses, and more.

In *Trust: The Social Virtues and the Creation of Prosperity*, Francis Fukuyama[17] argues that trust, transparency, and truth distinguish prosperous societies from struggling ones. If this is true on a national level, how much more so within families, businesses, and communities? While dishonesty may bring short-term gains, in the long run, it leads to decline.

## Overcoming the Temptation to Lie

How can we resist the urge to lie, especially when deception seems beneficial?

### *1. Take responsibility.*

Everyone has lied at some point, including the author of this book. The key is to recognize dishonesty for what it is, acknowledge its consequences, and take steps to change. Apologies must be sincere, not empty words to escape accountability.[18]

### *2. Slow down.*

Many lies stem from haste—making promises we cannot keep and exaggerating without thinking. I advise natural salespeople to write down their commitments, especially to their families, to ensure they are truthful. The phrase "less is more" is a valuable reminder: speaking less but with greater integrity builds credibility.

[17] Fukuyama, F. (1996). *Trust: The social virtues and the creation of prosperity*. Simon & Schuster.

[18] Miller, C. B., & West, R. (Eds.). (2020). *Integrity, honesty, and truth seeking*. Oxford University Press.

### *3. Be willing to take a hit in the short term.*

Lying might bring quick rewards—money, contracts, and prestige—but at what cost? In America, where personal identity and reputation are highly valued, maintaining integrity is far more important than short-term gains. The mentality of "now or never" might push people to justify deception. In reality, true opportunities rarely vanish forever. Staying honest and building a strong reputation will pay off in the long run.

### *4. Think long-term.*

Before speaking, ask, *how will this affect my character? My relationships? My reputation?* More importantly, *how will God evaluate me?* True success is not just financial—it is about who we become.

## Final Thoughts on Persuasiveness vs. Deception

Persuasiveness is crucial for success in any field. It shapes our careers, relationships, and influence. However, we must be mindful of the temptations that come with this ability.

While lying may seem harmless or even strategic, its consequences are severe. It weakens character, breeds insecurity, destroys trust, and ultimately leads to failure. True success comes from integrity. We must value our identity more than our possessions, prioritize truth over temporary gains, and always keep in mind the ultimate evaluation: God's judgment of our lives.

## Reflection and Discussion

*1. Where do I see this strength—and its shadow—in my own life?*

*2. What situations most often trigger the temptation connected to this strength?*

*3. What safeguards or disciplines can I put in place to cultivate the strength while resisting its temptation?*

*4. Who in my life models this strength well, and what can I learn from their example?*

# Further Reading

Carnegie & Associates, D. (2019). *Sell!: The way your customers want to buy*. G&D Media

Carnegie Training, D. (2011). *Stand and deliver: How to become a masterful communicator and public speaker*. Simon & Schuster.

Gallo, C. (2014). *Talk like TED: The 9 public-speaking secrets of the world's top minds*. St. Martin's Press.

Lowndes, L. (2003). *How to communicate with anyone: 92 little tricks for big success in relationships*. McGraw-Hill.

Nichols, M. P. (2009). *The lost art of listening: How learning to listen can improve relationships* (2nd ed.). Guilford Press.

Ognev, I., & Russev, V. (2017). *The psychology of communication*. CreateSpace Independent Publishing Platform.

Paterson, R. J. (2000). *The Assertiveness Workbook: How to Express Your Ideas and Stand Up for Yourself at Work and in Relationships*. New Harbinger Publications.

Pease, A., & Pease, B. (2004). *The definitive book of body language*. Bantam Books.

Seo, B. (2022). *The art of argument: How debate teaches us to listen and be heard*. Riverhead Books.

Sinek, S. (2009). *Start with why: How great leaders inspire everyone to take action*. Portfolio.

Voss, C., & Raz, T. (2016). *Never split the difference: Negotiating as if your life depended on it*. Harper Business.

Ziglar, Z. (1984). *Secrets of closing the sale*. Revell.

---

*Hard work can lead to success even in the absence of 'talent'.*

---

---

*Relying solely on talent without effort may NOT lead to success.*

---

# 3

# INDUSTRIOUSNESS VS. MATERIALISM

THE THIRD TRAIT I'VE NOTICED IN SUCCESSFUL PEOPLE is *industriousness*. The earlier you begin to develop it, the better. Industriousness is an intellectual muscle that must be trained. It both springs from and reinforces good habits. Industriousness is the engine that drives a person's dreams and ambitions, activating all other qualities. Few people rise to success without it, and those who do often lose everything quickly. Those who choose the difficult but fruitful path of hard work are rewarded in the long run.

Of course, even hard-working people are not immune to certain dangers. In this section, we'll examine one of the most pervasive threats of our age: *materialism*. I define materialism as an attempt to fulfill soul-deep needs with material resources. This isn't to say we don't need those resources—hunger is real—but the challenge is to succeed without being consumed by the disease of wealth accumulation.

## What Is Industriousness?

The meaning of industriousness is best seen not in the definition of the word but in its long-term outcomes. While a few studies suggest that periods of rest or unstructured time can support creativity, these findings refer to mental space rather than to chronic avoidance of effort. In other words, short intervals of idleness may spark insight, but sustained laziness rarely leads to innovation. Historically, and in most people's lived experience, consistent hard work produces progress, while the habitual avoidance of effort leads to stagnation rather than brilliance. Poverty has three main causes:

1. Unfavorable natural conditions like droughts, earthquakes, or illness.
2. Social injustice, including war, slavery, or systemic inequality.
3. Personal choices, such as laziness or self-pity, or destructive behaviors like substance abuse and crime.

No one is born industrious and hardworking. Everyone can find a reason to be lazy. The secret to success is choosing to work hard despite your circumstances.

In *The Protestant Ethic and the Spirit of Capitalism*, sociologist Max Weber asked why Europe and the United States dominated the world.[19] Here is part of the answer: a strong work ethic, grounded in self-discipline and purpose.

---

*History was not made by majorities, not even by minorities, but by personalities.*

---

## The Seven Marks of Industriousness

### *1. Adopt a sacrificial mindset.*

Industriousness begins with a willingness to sacrifice. It means giving up short-term pleasures—even legitimate needs—for the sake of higher goals. Someone once said, "Life is payment and play. If you

[19] Max Weber, *Protestant Ethics and the Spirit of Capitalism*, Antet XX Press, 2003.

play now, you pay later—with interest. But if you pay now, you get to play later—with dividends."

There's a temptation to "live in the moment," but the industrious person resists this pull. He knows that real life demands effort and that this investment will yield future rewards. The industrious person understands the vanity of this way of life, resists the current, and is willing to put in the effort necessary to be productive and learn because he knows this investment will pay off in the future.

Hard work also demands the courage to be in the minority, as most will try to do the minimum in any project. History, however, has not been made by majorities. If you want to be a successful person, you must be willing to sacrifice your own short-term desires and feelings to benefit from long-term success. As St. Paul said, "But I discipline my body and keep it under control, lest after preaching to others I myself should be disqualified" (1 Cor. 9:27).

### *2. Be disciplined.*

Discipline is doing what needs to be done, when it needs to be done, and even when you don't feel like it. Olympic athletes are a perfect example; they sacrifice leisure for years in pursuit of their goals. They accept responsibility and do hard things even if they are pushed outside their comfort zones. They are dedicated to doing unpleasant things if those things are important to reaching their goals.

I once worked as a telemarketer in the U.S., calling hundreds of people every day. With my Romanian accent, I was ridiculed often, hung up on even more, and faced a rejection rate that could crush anyone's confidence. My mentor noticed my hesitation and asked me one afternoon, "Sebastian, what do you do if you have to eat a frog?"

I stared at him in disbelief. "Eat a frog? Never!"

He smiled. "That's your problem. You waste time avoiding the inevitable. Me? I find the cleanest frog, season it with spices, and swallow it fast."

Only later did I understand what he meant. The frog was the practice of selling, the part of the job that felt humiliating, draining, and unavoidable. Every morning, I delayed picking up the phone because I feared another round of rejection. But avoiding it only made the day worse.

His lesson stayed with me: discipline means doing the hard thing first, quickly and without drama. For me, that meant dialing the phone before I felt ready, embracing the discomfort, and getting through the calls rather than letting them loom over me. Once I learned to "eat the frog," everything else in my day felt easier.

That is discipline: doing the hard thing, quickly and efficiently.

### *3. Work without supervision.*

True industriousness means working when no one is watching. It means you are not working for your boss or your teacher but for yourself. There's a saying, "He who works, works for himself; and he who gives, gives to himself." Successful people understand their greatest asset is themselves.

Christians believe that God "sees in secret" and rewards what is done faithfully when no one is watching. That perspective creates a powerful internal motivation for excellence and integrity because it anchors discipline in something deeper than external approval.

Scripture also teaches that God sometimes rewards openly, publicly affirming those who have been trustworthy in hidden places. Jesus' statement about being "faithful in small things" reminds us that self-management is not optional; it is the training ground for promotion, leadership, and greater responsibility. Whether the reward is quiet or visible, the principle remains the same: character is revealed in the private disciplines long before it is recognized in public.

### *4. Be efficient.*

Industriousness isn't about blind effort. It must be smart, strategic, and efficient. Someone once said, "If you work too hard, you won't have time to earn." In other words, hard work without strategy is self-defeating.

Since the 19th century, hundreds of machines and technologies have been invented to help farmers. Now, farmers are no longer manually planting acres of wheat, corn, etc. Tractors and farm machinery help in the whole process, making the farmers' work easier.

The same principle applies to the technology we can use in our work. As much as artificial intelligence (AI) technology scares us, it is a tool we can use to make our lives easier.

---

*Work smarter, not harder.*

---

Being industrious means achieving maximum results with minimum effort. This is what technology and creativity help us do. From communication to production, we have made enormous strides in the last century. Things that used to take hours are now done in minutes. However, in the 21st century, we are tempted to use technology primarily for fun and entertainment rather than for work. Successful people know how to augment their work with technology. Work efficiency requires a deep and detailed understanding of all the tools available. Often, the process of streamlining involves uncomfortable questions, changing methods or traditions, and painful trial-and-error. Successful people leverage technology rather than getting lost in it. They ask tough questions, experiment with new methods, and embrace discomfort in pursuit of greater efficiency.

### *5. Don't be a time-waster or a workaholic.*

There's a myth of busyness, often used to excuse a lack of productivity. A student says, "I didn't finish the project; I was too busy."

But a look at their screen time reveals hours lost to social media or Netflix. In *The Honest Truth About Dishonesty*, Dan Ariely wrote, "We're all very good at rationalizing our actions to fit our selfish motives." Most of us risk believing we've allocated enough time to a project, or we have wrong expectations about the effort required.

Another tendency is to be a *workaholic*, someone who works compulsively and is at risk of chronic stress, anxiety, and depression. This usually happens when someone is unsure of his or her own identity, believing they must work or sacrifice in order to gain the acceptance of others. People prone to workaholism can also be easily manipulated by unscrupulous individuals offering vague or unrealistic promises.

### *6. Set boundaries.*

Successful individuals understand that they cannot do everything, so they say "no" to trivialities and refuse to be manipulated by the tyranny of the urgent. They plan ahead and act preemptively to prevent crises. They are realistic with their resources—time, energy, and opportunities—and do not overpromise. Hardworking and industrious people think long-term and are willing to experience short-term losses rather than compromise or commit to something unrealistic.

Surprisingly, many of us find it easier to say "yes" and take on tasks without careful thought. Some are overly optimistic, assuming everything will go as planned with no setbacks or obstacles, but reality usually proves otherwise. Every project, sooner or later, runs into what was mentioned in a previous chapter, Murphy's Law, which states that if something can go wrong, it probably will, and at the worst time.

### *7. Delegate.*

Successful people know how to manage and delegate. Peter Drucker, the father of modern management, said, "Management is the art of accomplishing your objectives with the help of others."[20]

But delegation is not abdication. Unfortunately, many people only delegate tasks they dislike. That's why many managers and entrepreneurs constantly complain that they can't find good employees or lack reliable people to work with.

True delegation is about mentorship. It serves a short-term purpose—to get things done—but also a long-term one: to help the mentee grow into a capable professional. Delegation is rooted in altruism, loving your neighbor as yourself. It means treating your mentee as you would want to be treated. Successful people attract other talented individuals because of their wise and intentional delegation. The people around them are often willing to go the extra mile, even recommending others to become their mentees, because they have personally experienced growth and seen their environment flourish thanks to intelligent task delegation.

## Why Be Industrious?

I have friends and acquaintances, and have heard of others, who don't cultivate any of the traits described above and yet seem to be doing well. The extent to which they're "doing well" is debatable, but let's examine the arguments in favor of industriousness and hard work. You can then decide whether it's truly possible to succeed spiritually, materially, physically, or socially without it.

---

[20] Drucker, P. F., Collins, J. C., Kotler, P., Kouzes, J. M., Rodin, J., & Rangan, V. K. (2011). *The five most important questions you will ever ask about your organization.* Jossey-Bass.

### *1. In the long run, hard work is rewarded, while laziness is punished.*

There are some popular sayings like, "The early bird gets the worm, but the second mouse gets the cheese." Hardworking people are often seen as naïve or foolish, as if only the gullible are obedient, gracious, and consistent. Yes, diligent individuals can be manipulated, and sly people will always exist, but we must not let this discourage us from being hardworking. Industriousness pays off in the long run. Honest, hardworking people accumulate experience, skills, and a positive reputation. The habit of industriousness is like a snowball, as it grows with momentum. Tasks that seem daunting today will become easier over time if you stay focused.

I advise graduating students to become "stealable" employees, so hardworking and dedicated that other employers, clients, and competitors bid for their services. This doesn't happen overnight. It takes years of effort, commitment, and perseverance before recognition comes. You may feel overlooked, tired, or overwhelmed, but the rewards will follow. I've worked in business for over 30 years and have never met a diligent and hardworking person who regretted their hard work. Even when betrayed or exploited, they were able to change jobs easily, and their healthy habits went with them and were ultimately rewarded.

In contrast, lazy individuals, even if they managed to fake their way through for a while, were eventually exposed and discredited.

### *2. Industriousness builds habits.*

The second reason industriousness pays off is that it builds constructive habits. Habits are formed through repetition, as things we do consistently become easier. On the other hand, negative habits like gluttony, greed, apathy, anger, envy, or pride form effortlessly. Positive habits require effort and discipline.

Suppose you set a goal to read more. You buy books, start reading, and for the first week, it goes well. But to sustain the habit, you need perseverance. Over time, it will become easier to reach for a book instead of scrolling through social media. Reading, like other good habits, demands awareness, willpower, effort, and often resisting immediate gratification. While it may not feel as fun in the short term as watching a movie, it will sharpen your mind and make you more creative in the long run.

### *3. Experience brings wisdom.*

Industriousness and hard work not only sharpen your skills but also expand your understanding over time. Persistent effort leads to deeper insight into your craft, insight you wouldn't gain otherwise. This knowledge becomes a powerful tool for overcoming obstacles, whether internal or imposed by society. Experience allows you to surpass limits and help others do the same.

In *Outliers: The Story of Success*, Malcolm Gladwell[21] challenges the myth of innate genius. He shows that people like Mozart, Bill Gates, and The Beatles only reached exceptional levels after putting in over 10,000 hours in their fields. There are typically 2,080 work hours in a standard 40-hour workweek year, so 10,000 hours is equivalent to roughly five years of full-time work or a university degree. Yet many give up after just a week and wonder why they haven't "made it."

### *4. Industriousness attracts the right people.*

There's a saying, "Tell me who you're with, and I'll tell you who you are." Want to know who you are? Look at the people with whom you spend the most time. If you're surrounded by four fools, you're probably the fifth. But if you're surrounded by four successful people, chances are you're the fifth. Hustle attracts the right people and repels the wrong ones.

---

[21] Gladwell, M. (2008). *Outliers: The story of success*. Hachette Uk.

When you're consistent, serious, and dedicated, others notice. You earn respect and trust, build a solid reputation, and form deep, meaningful relationships. This network of like-minded individuals becomes your foundation, not just for achieving goals but for weathering tough times. The people around you will shape the quality of your spiritual, social, and material life.

### *5. Industriousness generates wealth.*

Finally, industriousness and hard work can generate wealth. By *wealth*, I don't mean greed or the love of money—which, as Scripture says, *is* "the root of all evil" (1 Tim. 6:10). However, we do need money to live. Supermarkets don't accept character as currency. Rent and bills are due regardless of your values. If you have a spouse, children, or parents, you are responsible for their well-being. Historically, hard work has been the most reliable path to financial security.

I've met many people who feed on dreams, gossip, and stories. They fantasize about luxury cars, perfect families, impressive houses, and exotic vacations but do little to attain them. They blame their teachers for poor grades, their bosses for low wages, and their government for their standard of living. While these institutions may be flawed, you and I cannot change them, but we can choose to be diligent and make the most of the opportunities we have.

## Materialism: The Temptation of Industrious People

So far, we've discussed the benefits of industriousness and hard work. But there's a temptation with hard work that must be acknowledged: materialism. The pursuit of wealth can easily become obsessive, and money can end up becoming the very thing that enslaves us.

If materialism were an image, it could be like a scene from the movie *Mean Girls,* in which four teenage girls are walking through the mall with their bags full of merchandise. The boys could be in the same picture with their longing for gadgets, technology, cars, cool clothes, etc. For adults, materialism could be represented by bigger houses, better cars, and exotic vacations. However materialism manifests itself, it reflects a deeper condition of the human soul. Increasingly present in people's lives, materialism has become a chief temptation of the 21st century.

Materialism is an attempt to fulfill spiritual needs with material things. Materialism is when material goods take hold of you, enslaving you to money and public opinion. The context in which we live is ripe for materialism. The economic growth of the last century has made such an impact on society that Harvard political scientist Samuel Huntington declared, "The triumphant religion of the 20th century was neither Christianity nor Islam, but economic growth."[22] This economic growth has given wings to materialism by producing a multitude of things society thinks it needs. We have television and social networks that present an idealized lifestyle, putting pressure on us to copy it.

I have encountered people—both poor and rich—who were consumed by materialism. I've met poor individuals who dreamed of wealth to the point of despair and wealthy individuals who feared losing their fortune so much that they lived joyless, paranoid lives. Materialism has little to do with how much you have. It has everything to do with what has you.

## What Does Materialism Look Like?

Materialism affects every human being, but I have noticed that hardworking people are tempted by materialism in a special way. It shows up when:

---

[22] Huntington, S. P. (2011). *The clash of civilizations and the remaking of world order*. Simon & Schuster.

- We can't rest because we're always chasing more.
- We define our self-worth by our possessions.
- We envy others' success, believing we're less because we have less.
- We spend more than we make, just to keep up appearances.
- We measure our value by the size of our house, our income, our social media following, or our lifestyle.

Industriousness and hard work—when untethered from values like humility, generosity, and contentment—turn into greed. The tragedy is that materialistic people often don't realize they're enslaved. They appear successful on the outside but are tormented within—anxious, isolated, and never satisfied.

Materialism creates fragile identities. If your sense of self is built on what you own, a downturn in the market, a job loss, or even someone else's success can shake your entire foundation. This is why Jesus teaches us in Matthew 6:19–21,

> Do not store up for yourselves treasures on earth, where moth and rust destroy, and where thieves break in and steal. But store up for yourselves treasures in heaven. For where your treasure is, there your heart will be also.

This doesn't mean we shouldn't own anything or that wealth is inherently wrong. It means we must own things without letting those things own *us*. From my observations and research, materialism manifests itself in three ways.

## The Three Manifestations of Materialism

### *1. The Lust of the Eyes*

This is living at a purely visual level and only caring about things that look impressive. The lust of the eyes is drawn to what glitters and dazzles, blurring the line between needs and wants, often justifying one's appetite for luxury. It causes a person to covet everything in the store windows.

### *2. The Indulgence of Animal Instincts*

I've had the opportunity to travel in the UK, and I think the British have mastered etiquette and public image. What intrigued me was what happens after work hours, when appearances no longer matter. I remember visiting the university campus in Oxford. By day, it was a symbol of British intellect and refinement. However, at night, it transformed into a bastion of intoxicated, disorderly revelry. It seemed as though, after a day of restraint, people needed to release all their primal urges.

### *3. Boasting*

We boast about our dreams and accomplishments, unaware that we may offend those around us. Even more, in our pride, we often forget those who helped us succeed and, above all, God, who gave us life, breath, and being. Boasting may draw praise in public, but behind closed doors, it often invites gossip, ridicule, and envy.

I've spent years traveling to major cities across the U.S. for business—places like Atlanta, Dallas, and Chicago. In many of these cities, you'll find business districts sprouting up near airports, designed for convenience and international access. Take, for example, the booming developments in northern Dallas along the Tollway or the area around Buckhead in Atlanta. Skyscrapers, tech offices, and co-working hubs stretch for blocks. But I've often walked those streets and felt something strange, like the deeper purpose behind capitalism had gotten lost. Eventually, these office districts all seemed to get their own version of the same thing: a high-end mall. In the middle of the corporate sprawl, you'll find places like The Shops at Legacy or Lenox Square, full of designer boutiques, upscale coffee shops, and restaurants with valet parking. Now, before heading into work, some people swing by to grab their Starbucks or browse the latest at Burberry. It's like they need a reminder: *This is what you're working for*. Long hours, tight deadlines, and pressure-filled jobs—all to fuel the next purchase.

Don't get me wrong; I'm not against malls or brand names. I firmly believe that hard work, creativity, and effort should be rewarded. But the danger comes when we try to satisfy our souls with material things alone. That's when the system starts to feel hollow.

## Why Is Materialism Dangerous?

You might look at industrious and successful people and conclude that their lives are perfect.[23] There is nothing wrong with having possessions, especially when acquired through honest work. In the beginning, materialism feels pleasant. But with time, it disappoints. Some of its promises turn out to be illusions. Here are some reasons why materialism is dangerous.

### *1. Temptation to bypass effort and integrity—to get things without earning them.*

I call this the lottery phenomenon. I've seen it again and again: people who began with honesty and diligence are later derailed by flashy role models, choosing shortcuts and schemes. Why stay committed when your old classmate joined a political party and now heads a state-owned company? Deep within us lurks the disturbing

---

[23] Tim Kasser, *The high price of materialism*, MIT Press, 2003.

impulse to keep only the rewards of honesty while skipping its process and price.

### *2. The risk of loving things and using people.*

True, lasting success means loving people and using things—not the reverse. I've seen hardworking people who, after achieving success, sacrificed their relationships. They went from being generous mentors to manipulators and deceivers. During World War II, Churchill was asked about Great Britain's friendship with the Soviet Union. Smiling, he said, "Gentlemen, countries don't have friends, they don't even have allies—they only have interests." It's tragic when this mindset is applied not only to geopolitics but also to human relationships.

### *3. The risk of neglecting our health—not just physically but especially mentally.*

People who work relentlessly without inner peace, driven by public opinion and constant comparison, are destined to burn out. St. Paul described it vividly:

> Those who desire to be rich fall into temptation and are ensnared by many foolish and harmful desires that plunge people into ruin and destruction. For the love of money is the root of all kinds of evil. Some, in pursuing it, have wandered from the faith and pierced themselves with many sorrows. (1 Tim. 6:9–10)

### *3. The risk of sacrificing our family and community.*

Sooner or later, those who try to fill their souls with material things begin to neglect themselves and those closest to them. They may hurt their loved ones and damage their reputation, ending up surrounded only by opportunists.

*The Great Gatsby* offers a poignant example of materialism's destructiveness. Jay Gatsby acquired his wealth dishonestly, a textbook case of the lottery phenomenon, and surrounds himself with superficial friends and freeloaders. From the outside, their lifestyle appears ideal: no work, constant pleasure, and moral looseness. Yet no one is truly happy. Gatsby himself longs for something greater:

> . . . he stretched out his arms toward the dark water with a curious gesture, and, far as I was from him, I could have sworn he was trembling. Involuntarily I glanced seaward—and distinguished nothing except a single green light, minute and far away.[24]

Gatsby's lonely death is a stark warning to anyone willing to see through the illusion. "For what does it profit a man to gain the whole world and forfeit his soul?" (Mark 8:36).

## The Antidote to Materialism: Sustainable Altruism

Since materialism is so dangerous and wreaks havoc on our lives, relationships, and health, is there an antidote? Some people wrongly recommend laziness or poverty as a cure for materialism, a kind of withdrawal from society or an abdication of responsibility. I often come across documentaries that glorify simple country life or living in the mountains or jungle, presented as the purest way to live. There's nothing wrong with simplicity, and if you feel called to a rural lifestyle, that's great. But it's important to have a full picture of what such a life entails, not just its benefits but also its inherent hardships and limitations.

We are called to live in the modern world as "salt and light," to influence and enrich our communities through our own example.

---

[24] Fitzgerald, F. Scott (Francis Scott), 1896-1940. (1925). *The great Gatsby*. New York: C. Scribner's sons.

Honesty must be cultivated not only for our own well-being but also for the good of others, and it should be balanced with sustainable altruism. From what I've observed, experienced, and studied in many successful individuals, it truly is more blessed to give than to receive. The Christian ethic that helped build Europe is encapsulated in this admonition from John Wesley: "Earn as much as you can, save as much as you can, and give as much as you can."

## The Four Components of Altruism

### *1. Concrete Numbers and Specific Goals*

Altruism is sustainable only through having specific goals. Materialism, on the other hand, thrives on moving targets and vague aspirations. Ask someone how much money they want, and most will say, "As much as possible." Ask how big their house should be, and the answer will likely be "a decent size" or "as big as possible." Where would they like to go on vacation? "Somewhere nice." The issue with moving targets is that you never know if you've reached your goal. You risk being perpetually dissatisfied. No matter your situation, someone is doing better—or worse—than you. You must choose whether to be content or discontent.

A journalist once asked John D. Rockefeller, the richest man of his time, "Mr. Rockefeller, you're a multi-billionaire. How much more money do you need to be content?"

After pausing for a moment, Rockefeller replied, "Just a little more."

That's why I recommend writing down specific goals: your ideal monthly income, the square footage of your home, the kind of car you want to drive, and—most importantly—how much you want to save for retirement.

### *2. Attitude of Temperance and the Discipline to Save*

I suggest learning to live on 70 percent of your income. Allocate 10 percent to charitable giving, 10 percent to passive investments, and 10 percent to active investments. What you invest in isn't as important as cultivating the mindset of temperance and generosity. If living on 70 percent of your income feels impossible, it may be time to consider changing jobs—or even starting a business. Once that 70 percent becomes a meaningful amount, consider using part of it for philanthropy.

### *3. Intellectual Generosity*

When people think of generosity, they usually think of money. And while financial giving is important, I believe intellectual generosity is even more so. This means sharing knowledge and habits, especially from successful people, with those who are less privileged. It includes offering opportunities for growth and employment, not just short-term financial help. Financial handouts often foster dependency, self-pity, and even manipulation. Meanwhile, the giver can fall into the trap of a superiority complex and ego inflation.

Consider the contrast between Africa and China over recent decades.[25] In the late 1970s, both regions faced dire poverty and famine. Without delving into political complexities, we can observe that China benefited from generous intellectual investment and opportunities to manufacture for Western markets. Africa, in contrast, mostly received financial aid aimed at consumption. Today, Europe welcomes tourists from China and refugees from Africa.

---

[25] Schell, O., & Delury, J. (2014). *Wealth and power: China's long march to the twenty-first century*. Random House Trade Paperbacks.

### *4. Financial Generosity*

Yes, giving money has its risks—for both donor and recipient—but true philanthropy remains a deeply benevolent act. For those who have found financial success, giving is a way to resist greed and materialism. It is a declaration that what we have is not entirely ours and that we are merely stewards. It offers a powerful way to serve those suffering from circumstances beyond their control, such as illness, disability, disaster, or systemic oppression like corruption and discrimination.

In this chapter, we have emphasized industriousness as the third trait of successful people. We've explored the question, "What is wealth, and why does it matter?" We've examined materialism—its seductive pull and dangers—and proposed sustainable altruism as a meaningful and fulfilling alternative.

In the next chapter, we'll turn our focus to creativity, the fourth trait of successful people, which often comes paired with its own temptation: dissatisfaction.

## Reflection and Discussion

*1. Where do I see this strength—and its shadow—in my own life?*

*2. What situations most often trigger the temptation connected to this strength?*

*3. What safeguards or disciplines can I put in place to cultivate the strength while resisting its temptation?*

*4. Who in my life models this strength well, and what can I learn from their example?*

---

*Put in the hard work today*
*to reap the great rewards tomorrow.*

---

## Further Reading

Abdaal, A. (2023). *Feel-good productivity: How to achieve more of what matters to you*. Ebury Edge.

Allen, D. (2001). *Getting things done: The art of stress-free productivity*. Penguin Books.

Barringer, B. R., & Ireland, R. D. (2015). *Entrepreneurship: Successfully launching new ventures* (5th ed.). Pearson.

Burkett, L. (2006). *Business by the book: The complete guide of biblical principles for the workplace*. Thomas Nelson.

Clear, J. (2018). *Atomic habits: Tiny changes, remarkable results: An easy & proven way to build good habits & break bad ones*. Avery.

Collins, J., & Lazier, B. (2020). *BE 2.0 (Beyond Entrepreneurship 2.0): Turning your business into an enduring great company*. Portfolio.

Duhigg, C. (2016). *Smarter faster better: The secrets of being productive in life and business*. Random House.

Hisrich, R. D., Peters, M. P., & Shepherd, D. A. (2016). *Entrepreneurship* (10th ed.). McGraw-Hill Education.

Kuratko, D. F. (2016). *Entrepreneurship: Theory, process, and practice* (10th ed.). Cengage Learning

Sinek, S. (2014). *Leaders eat last: Why some teams pull together and others don't*. Portfolio.

Tracy, B. (2016). *Just shut up and do it: 7 steps to conquer your goals*. Simple Truths.

Weber, M. (2001). *The Protestant ethic and the spirit of capitalism*. Routledge.

Wickman, G., & Bouwer, T. (2017). *What the heck is EOS?: A complete guide for employees in companies running on EOS*. BenBella Books.

---

*Invest your time wisely.*
*It's the only resource you*
*can't replenish.*

---

# 4

# CREATIVITY VS. DISSATISFACTION

THE FOURTH TRAIT I HAVE NOTICED IN SUCCESSFUL people is creativity, which is the engine of progress. Creativity is both an art and a science that finds innovative solutions to real-world problems.

Creative people possess a heightened sense of realism and innovation. On one hand, they see the world as it is; on the other hand, they can imagine and implement solutions for a better world. They have an unconstrained, outside-the-box, problem-solving mindset that generates possible solutions to seemingly impossible situations. These individuals perceive things others might miss and see potential where others see only obstacles.

In this chapter, we will explore the importance of creativity and offer practical tools to develop it, a vital element for success. We also examine the inherent temptation for creative individuals to be perpetually dissatisfied.

We conclude the chapter with recommendations for channeling discontent constructively so it does not undermine what we build through creativity.

## What Is Creativity?

One common misconception is to associate creativity with strangeness or eccentricity. Creativity is not about inventing bizarre concepts merely for the sake of being different. Some believe the more unusual or absurd an idea is, the more creative it must be. But being creative is not about shocking people or breaking conventions just to stand out, nor is it about wearing unusual clothes or expressing eccentricity for its own sake. Creativity is not proposing unrealistic solutions disconnected from reality; it should ultimately lead to order and improvement. It is not about rejecting tradition without cause or reinventing the wheel with every project.

As we shall see, creativity often involves combining existing ideas in new and meaningful ways. Finally, creativity is not a magical, instantaneous flash of genius. True creativity involves dedicated effort, perseverance, and the willingness to refine ideas over time. Let's explore some characteristics of creative people.

### *1. Adaptability*

The first characteristic of creative people is adaptability. They keep pace with changes in their industries and in society at large. They are typically flexible and open to new ideas, consistently striving to adjust their approach as circumstances evolve. For them, change is not a threat but an opportunity for growth and innovation.

A prime example is Jeff Bezos, founder of Amazon. He demonstrated adaptability when he decided to evolve the company from an online bookstore into a massive e-commerce platform. Faced with changing market conditions, he expanded into new categories such as cloud computing (AWS) and digital streaming. Bezos' ability to adapt Amazon's business model in response to technological advances and shifting consumer needs was crucial to its exponential growth through diversification.

---

*Creativity is both an art and a science in which you find innovative solutions to real-world problems.*

---

### *2. Ingenuity*

The second characteristic of creative people is ingenuity. Beyond being adaptable, creative individuals make the most of the resources available to them. While many attribute success solely to having resources, creative people thrive even when resources are limited. In contrast to mediocre individuals who blame failure on a lack of means, creative people excel by finding innovative solutions regardless of constraints. They have an exceptional talent for reusing existing resources or ideas, choosing to see opportunities where others see only problems. There are no problems—only opportunities!

An inspiring example of creative ingenuity is Howard Schultz, the visionary behind Starbucks. Raised in a poor housing complex in Brooklyn, Schultz grew up watching his father struggle in low-paying jobs with no benefits. This shaped his vision for a company where employees—whom he calls "partners"—would be treated with dignity. With no wealth or powerful connections, Schultz took a small coffee chain and reimagined it as a global "third place" between work and home. His ingenuity wasn't just in the business model; it was in his ability to create culture, elevate everyday experiences, and prove that business could serve both people and profit. His story is a powerful reminder that creative ingenuity can transform not only industries but also individual lives.

Elon Musk, the South African-born entrepreneur, exemplifies ingenuity. At Tesla, he transformed the electric vehicle industry by developing high-performance, long-range cars that many thought impossible. His innovative thinking also extended to SpaceX, where he pioneered reusable rocket technology, dramatically reducing the cost of space travel. Musk's ingenious solutions have disrupted multiple industries and redefined what is possible.

### *3. Vision*

The third characteristic of creative people is vision. They have an extraordinary ability to see with the mind's eye what does not yet exist. One of my favorite quotes about vision is "Now faith [vision] is confidence in what we hope for and assurance about what we do not see" (Heb. 11:1). Where others see dead ends, creative individuals see new possibilities. They nurture a capacity to imagine the future. Everyone is gifted with vision, yet many allow theirs to be distorted by negative experiences, which transform vision into fear. By contrast, creative people cultivate a visionary mindset fueled by willpower, enabling them to push past boundaries and generate original ideas.

Steve Jobs, founder of Apple, is a perfect example. Jobs' vision transformed Apple into a tech giant. He foresaw the value of user-friendly personal computers, intuitive mobile devices, and an integrated digital ecosystem. His foresight led to groundbreaking products such as the Macintosh, iPod, iPhone, and iPad. Jobs' visions even extended to retail, as seen in the innovative Apple Store concept that revolutionized how consumers interact with technology.

### *4. Optimism*

The fourth characteristic of creative people is optimism. From both research and personal observation, I have found that creatives tend to succeed because they maintain a positive outlook even in adversity. This optimism fuels persistence. Creative people view setbacks as temporary and solvable, allowing them to press forward when others would give up.

People tend to fall into one of two broad categories: optimists and pessimists. Optimists perceive life as a generally positive experience, occasionally disrupted by negative events. Pessimists, on the other hand, see life as a generally negative experience, interrupted now and then by something positive. When an optimist faces hardship or injustice, they think, "No problem; life will return to its positive state!" When a pessimist encounters something good, they say, "Don't get too excited; it won't last too long." Sadly, these beliefs often become self-fulfilling prophecies.

## *5. Problem-Solving*

The fifth characteristic of creative people is that they are problem solvers. Rather than becoming stuck, they actively and diligently pursue solutions. They are curious and enjoy the intellectual challenge of resolving complex issues. They often approach problems from multiple angles, merging ideas across disciplines to generate creative solutions. They don't shy away from hard work and understand that solutions often emerge through persistent trial-and-error. While many complain or look for someone to blame, successful individuals roll up their sleeves and get to work.

Reed Hastings, co-founder of Netflix, exemplifies this. Frustrated by late fees from video rental stores, he launched a DVD-by-mail service. As technology evolved, he solved the problem of limited content distribution by shifting to online streaming. Later, to address content scarcity, Netflix began producing original programming, becoming a dominant force in entertainment.

Another great example is Ingvar Kamprad, the Swedish entrepreneur who founded IKEA. In the 1950s, Kamprad faced a major challenge: the cost of shipping fully assembled furniture was sky-high, making it hard to offer affordable prices to the average consumer. Solving this problem became his primary goal.

Then came the spark. He noticed an employee struggling to fit a table into a car. The employee suggested taking the legs off to make it easier. That simple idea triggered a revolution. Kamprad realized that, if customers assembled furniture themselves and the products were packed flat, it would dramatically reduce shipping costs and storage space. This seemingly small change turned into flat-pack furniture, a concept that became the cornerstone of IKEA's global success. Kamprad's ability to see a solution where others saw inconvenience turned IKEA into one of the most recognizable and beloved home furnishing brands in the world. Today, IKEA operates in over 60 countries and sells millions of products every year, many of them still flat-packed.

### *6. Focus on the Future*

The sixth characteristic of creative individuals is that they are focused on the future. Present circumstances are largely determined by past actions or inactions. If we want to shape tomorrow, we must act today. Creative people work with the future in mind. This forward-looking perspective drives their innovation and creativity.

In his book *The 7 Habits of Highly Effective People,*[26] Stephen Covey emphasizes the value of being future-focused. He describes successful people as those who visualize the end of a project before they begin—like an architect imagining a building before laying its foundation.

### *7. Involvement*

The seventh trait of creative people is involvement. They are engaged, present, and actively participating in the world around them. They are keen observers, continually absorbing ideas and information. This involvement allows them to draw inspiration from a variety of sources and make surprising connections.

A powerful example of this trait is Yvon Chouinard, the founder of Patagonia, the outdoor clothing and gear company. Chouinard didn't just start a business; he lived his brand. A passionate climber and environmentalist, he built Patagonia around his own lifestyle and values. His deep involvement in nature and environmental causes shaped every aspect of the company, from the durable, eco-conscious products to the company's activist stance on sustainability and ethical sourcing. His involvement wasn't limited to product design; he committed Patagonia to donating 1 percent of its sales to environmental causes and later transferred ownership of the company to a trust to ensure that its profits support environmental protection perpetually. His immersive approach—blending passion,

---

[26] Covey, S. R. (2014). *The 7 habits of highly effective people: Interactive edition.* FranklinCovey Co.

purpose, and business—created a company that not only thrives economically but also inspires globally.

### *8. Leadership*

The eighth and final trait is leadership. Leadership is initiative and influence. A leader is someone who takes the first step, takes risks, puts in the work, and isn't afraid of embarrassment. Leadership is also about cultivating influence to engage others in solving problems. Sadly, many want the benefits of leadership without the cost. True leadership requires humility and self-development. If you believe you're all-knowing and never admit ignorance, you're unlikely to learn or grow. You may instead spend your energy defending your views or hiding your lack of knowledge.

Creative leaders ask questions, seek input, and invest in their own growth.

Bill Gates' dedication to lifelong learning exemplifies this. As a young man, he taught himself multiple programming languages. At Microsoft, he stayed ahead of trends through constant learning. After stepping away from Microsoft, he broadened his knowledge to address global challenges through the Gates Foundation, applying his creativity to health and education issues.

Creativity is essential for success in the 21st century. The good news is that, regardless of our natural abilities, we can all cultivate creativity through discipline and curiosity. Successful people understand that creativity drives progress. They know how to channel it into problem-solving and resilience.

Yet with great creativity often comes the temptation of dissatisfaction. In the next section, we will examine this tendency and explore how to neutralize it constructively.

## Destructive Discontent: The Temptation of Creative People

The starting point of creativity is constructive dissatisfaction. Successful people look at the current state of things and imagine what they could become. In essence, it is a dissatisfaction with the status quo that is transformed into one's own vision (creativity) through sustained effort and discipline (hard work). However, uncontrolled dissatisfaction can be destructive; it becomes dangerous when it can no longer be contained—when we are constantly dissatisfied with the results. We have all had times when we were unhappy with how things turned out. We have all encountered circumstances that did not meet our expectations, or we have been deceived by those around us. In such moments, we experience the negative emotions, frustrations, and anxieties that come with dissatisfaction. Dissatisfaction is a state of unease, annoyance, or displeasure that occurs when something does not unfold as we expect. While it can motivate change, it can also be a source of deep frustration and negativity.

## Where Does Destructive Discontent Come From?

To manage dissatisfaction, it is essential to understand its roots.

### 1. *We live in an imperfect reality.*[27]

Despite our best efforts, the natural state of the world leans toward disorder. This is evident everywhere. The desire to look for solutions can slowly turn into the satisfaction of merely finding faults.

[27] Craib, I. (1994). *The importance of disappointment*. Routledge. https://doi.org/10.4324/9780203422236.

---

*The desire to look for solutions can slowly turn into the satisfaction of merely finding faults.*

---

This is exemplified by the presence of weeds. Whether it's an agricultural field, the lawn of a luxurious residence, or the vegetable garden of an average household, weeds will overrun the place if not regularly removed. Anything left in its natural state tends to deteriorate. Consider a brand-new house left untouched for 10 years; will it get better or worse with time?

In this imperfect, thorny, and challenging world, the seeds of discontent can easily sprout. As we strive for better, we become acutely aware of the gap between what is and what could be. The desire to seek solutions can devolve into a compulsion to find flaws. Creativity turns to cynicism, inventiveness is used for revenge, and we risk spinning in an endless cycle of frustration. We become blind to past achievements and fixate on an imperfect present that stifles our creativity.

### *2. We desire perfection.*

From my own observations and reflections, every human being has a grain of perfection etched into their DNA. Deep in our hearts is the notion of paradise. Perfectionism—wanting everything to be flawless—can be a virtue. But without a healthy understanding and clear boundaries, it becomes a dangerous trap.

Perfectionists live in a world of perpetual dissatisfaction. Every achievement, no matter how significant, falls short of an unattainable ideal. No result is good enough. No person measures up. We look in the mirror and see our flaws. We look at those around us and see their imperfections. We work in flawed companies, live in flawed cities, and worship in flawed churches. Rather than improving them, we consume images of a perfect but unreal world. One of the most dangerous examples is pornography. Magazines and websites promote a false, unattainable reality, setting unrealistic expectations. Others become absorbed in soap operas or movies that portray a polished world far removed from daily life. Social media takes it even further, showcasing friends and acquaintances with seemingly perfect lives.

### *3. We battle pride.*

Proud people believe they are the center of the universe and are constantly frustrated when others fail to recognize them. They are convinced that no one is worthy of them. As noted in Chapter 2, pride is the most dangerous of the seven deadly sins. This inflated self-image creates a belief in one's inherent superiority, that one is deserving of special treatment and immunity from the common difficulties of life. This mindset produces a toxic form of dissatisfaction rooted in the belief that the world fails to acknowledge their exceptionalism properly. Every interaction, collaboration, or relationship becomes a potential disappointment because reality can never meet their expectations.

Instead of channeling creativity toward progress, the proud and dissatisfied person lives in a parallel world. They believe they have all the answers yet feel restricted, misunderstood, betrayed, or undervalued. They fall prey to conspiracy theories—i.e., "the die is already cast"—while ignoring their own faults. Pride fosters a false sense of infallibility, stunting both personal and professional growth. When failures inevitably occur, the proud person is unequipped to handle them. Ultimately, pride not only fuels dissatisfaction but undermines the success it so desperately seeks, leading to isolation, stagnation, and unfulfilled potential.

## What Does Destructive Discontent Look Like?

### *1. Contempt*

Destructive and uncontrolled dissatisfaction manifests itself first as contempt. Creativity turns to arrogance and boastfulness. No one and nothing are exempt—especially those in positions of authority or prominence. Collaboration becomes nearly impossible, as the discontent person believes no one matches their talent or insight. This dismissiveness either leads to isolation or surrounds them with sycophants, people who laugh at all their jokes and celebrate all their achievements without genuine conviction.

### *2. Excessive Criticism*

Destructive dissatisfaction is marked by excessive criticism without offering solutions. While critical thinking can be constructive, this behavior quickly becomes corrosive. Creative individuals who fall into this trap may start out with good intentions, seeking improvement and excellence, but gradually shift their focus entirely to flaws, both real and imagined. Everything becomes a target for scrutiny, and time and energy are drained by endless critiques and postmortems. Achievements are minimized or forgotten altogether.

This can be especially damaging to teams, families, and close relationships. Those close to the critical creative person may feel constantly under attack, becoming defensive or withdrawn. The environment becomes one of fear and reluctance to share ideas. Innovation suffers as people focus more on avoiding criticism than contributing solutions.

---

*A disturbing manifestation of this dissatisfaction is the compromise of values in pursuit of quick fixes.*

---

### 3. Constant Complaining

Destructive dissatisfaction shows itself in constant complaining, innuendo, gossip, or flattery. This negativity contaminates both personal mindsets and institutional cultures. Time and energy are wasted voicing grievances without offering constructive solutions. Most of us justify our complaints as being about "real issues" and rarely admit when we're complaining. We say we are "discussing," "highlighting," or "bringing attention to problems." I have witnessed countless meetings where participants believed that intense discussions alone could solve problems.

This behavior poisons relationships and organizational environments.[28] Voicing dissatisfaction without proposing solutions creates a contagious negativity that erodes morale and productivity. Eventually, people may lose motivation altogether, feeling that no matter what they do, it won't be enough. Complaining, gossiping, and flattery become self-fulfilling prophecies, draining emotional energy and even harming physical health. Someone once said, "The truck that brings money to the bank is silent, while the truck that picks up garbage wakes up the whole street."

### 4. Unethical or Illegal Behavior

A disturbing expression of frustration is compromising values for short-term gain. This happens when, frustrated by slow progress or unforeseen obstacles, we begin to justify cutting corners. Didn't study for the exam? Cheat. Lacking a competitive edge? Bribe someone. Sadly, such behaviors are often reinforced by those around us: "This is just how it works," "You have no choice," and "Everyone's doing it." Before long, we're caught up in unethical or even criminal acts.

---

[28] Pallotta, D. (2010, October 14). Gossip kills possibility. *Harvard Business Review.* https://hbr.org/2010/10/gossip-kills-possibility.

Someone on this path might engage in tax evasion, fraud, bribery, labor law violations, employee exploitation, anti-competitive behavior, environmental violations, or intellectual property theft. The consequences can be devastating, from fines and imprisonment to bankruptcy and permanent damage to reputation. Even if undiscovered, the psychological toll is immense. Instead of building value through excellence and creativity, one spends energy hiding wrongdoing.

## Why Is Destructive Discontent Dangerous?

In my research and experience, most people don't recognize dissatisfaction as a serious problem. They see it in others and occasionally acknowledge it in themselves, while taking no steps to address it. Before offering solutions, I'd like to underline the dangers of unchecked dissatisfaction.

### *1. Perfectionism can become paralyzing.*

Some perfectionists fear failure so much that they procrastinate. Projects remain forever in the "draft" stage. When they do perform tasks, they are haunted by anxiety and fear that their work isn't good enough. This mindset stifles innovation and joy. Fear of criticism leads to risk aversion, which leads to missed opportunities. Perfectionism drains the joy from life.

I had a student who was brilliant and creative but also a perfectionist. He dreamed of the ideal situation: a flawless team working on a world-changing product. He was intensely bothered by the imperfections of others, frequently accusing his teammates of lacking integrity. He had outstanding ideas and generous funding from both domestic and international sources. Sadly, he has neither started a business nor joined a reputable organization. His impact remains limited because perfectionism paralyzes him. Such great potential wasted by perfectionism.

### *2. Dissatisfaction damages relationships.*

Those caught in its grip—obsessed with flaws and micromanagement—alienate friends, colleagues, and loved ones. They exude distrust, undervalue others, and exhaust even the most supportive partners. Frequent changes and broken promises are interpreted as flakiness or even malice. Eventually, people drift away, and reputations suffer.

### *3. Dissatisfaction leads to missed opportunities.*

When our vision is clouded by complaints and negativity, we overlook the valuable. We may abandon good projects or relationships simply because they fall short of perfection. The inability to celebrate small wins leads to the rejection of otherwise promising paths.

### *4. Dissatisfaction leads to burnout.*

Chronic discontent is emotionally and mentally exhausting. The pursuit of impossible standards, self-criticism, and refusal to celebrate success creates a breeding ground for exhaustion and breakdown. Even if we achieve something, we are too weighed down by perceived flaws to enjoy it.

In their landmark *Harvard Business Review* article,[29] "Manage Your Energy, Not Your Time," Tony Schwartz and Catherine McCarthy offer practical tools to align physical, emotional, mental, and spiritual energy. They echo what Solomon once said: "Above all else, guard your heart, for everything you do flows from it" (Prov. 4:23).

Like gasoline, dissatisfaction can be a powerful fuel for success. It can drive us to innovate, improve, and take bold risks. But, like oil, it can also burn us out, damaging our health, relationships, and

---

[29] Schwartz, T., & McCarthy, C. (2007). Manage your energy, not your time. *Harvard Business Review*, 85(10), 63–73.

character. In the next section, I will share solutions to tame and redirect dissatisfaction constructively.

## The Antidote to Discontent: Embracing Loss

Expert studies consistently highlight that the secret to success in any endeavor is balance. If you've read carefully, you've likely noticed this theme woven throughout the principles we've explored so far. A good friend of mine, whose father was a professional driver, once shared a piece of advice his father often gave: "Every road lies between two ditches." A good driver doesn't swerve left or right but remains centered. So it is with life: balance between what we want and what we have, between expectations and achievements, between dissatisfaction and creative drive.

One of the most powerful antidotes to discontent is learning to embrace loss—not as failure but as a natural and even necessary part of the journey. Embracing loss doesn't mean we stop caring or that pain disappears. It means we're no longer enslaved by outcomes or controlled by fear. It means we hold success and failure loosely, resting in the belief that something greater is at work—even in our setbacks.

To embrace loss is to relinquish control and pride. It is to acknowledge that our worth and destiny are not solely defined by what we build, win, or accomplish. To illustrate this principle, let's look at three ancient kings: Saul, David, and Absalom.

---

*Embracing loss does not mean embracing failure; it means renouncing control and pride.*

---

## The Story of Three Kings

Gene Edwards' *A Tale of Three Kings*[30] paints a vivid portrait of three biblical leaders, each representing a different response to ambition, power, and loss.

King Saul, the first to be anointed, had every natural advantage: height, charisma, strength, and leadership. But he became overconfident in his own power and began to make decisions fueled by fear, jealousy, and dissatisfaction. He eventually unraveled, choosing to protect his position at all costs, even if it meant unethical acts and alienating those closest to him.

In contrast, David, the shepherd boy turned giant slayer, had every opportunity to fight back and seize power when Saul disqualified himself. But instead, David chose the wilderness. He lost his title, status, and safety yet did not lose his integrity. David understood a profound truth: God's timing matters more than human ambition. His refusal to take the kingdom by force was not weakness; it was wisdom and ultimately the reason he was exalted.

Absalom, David's own son, stands in stark contrast. Impatient, critical, and burning with ambition, Absalom couldn't tolerate delay or disappointment. He plotted against his own father, leading a rebellion driven by pride and a hunger for power. But his refusal to embrace loss became his undoing. His story reminds us that unchecked ambition—especially when rooted in unresolved discontent—can destroy everything, including the person who harbors it.

The stories of these three kings speak volumes about our own struggles. They show that embracing loss is not a call to passivity or weakness but to surrender and trust. As the Apostle Peter writes,

> Therefore, humble yourselves under the mighty hand of God, that He may exalt you in due time, casting all your care upon Him, for He cares for you. (1 Pet. 5:5-7)

---

[30] Edwards, G. (2011). *A tale of three kings: A study in brokenness*. Tyndale House Publishers.

For those of us who face discontent, this embrace of loss offers a liberating perspective. True fulfillment and success can exist alongside loss, defeat, illness, and disappointment. Fulfillment and success are enabled by the ability to remain content and active even when we fall short of our primary goal, even when the earth gives us thorns and thistles as a reward for our hard work. The example of the three kings invites us to consider whether our dissatisfaction stems not from external circumstances but from our insistence on holding tight to our own expectations and desires.

Embracing loss is not about giving up on your goals or settling for mediocrity. It's about redefining success and contentment. Sometimes giving up control or immediate results can open the door to unexpected opportunities and growth. The road to success is often counterintuitive. In a world that glorifies winning at all costs, the ability to embrace loss—to relinquish the need for control, let go of control over outcomes, and prioritize integrity over immediate gain—can be the key that opens the door to true satisfaction.

## How to Embrace Loss Without Losing Yourself

What does it look like to embrace loss in the real world? How can we respond to failure, disappointment, and change in a way that fuels—not derails—our success? Here are four practical strategies:

### *1. Learn to pivot without shame.*

Sometimes success requires a change in direction. Pivoting is not failure; it's wisdom. It's the courageous decision to change course when something isn't working.[31] I experienced this firsthand in college. Pressured by family expectations, I started out in medical school only to discover two years in that I lacked both the passion

[31] Arteaga, R., & Hyland, J. (2013). *Pivot: How top entrepreneurs adapt and change course to find ultimate success.* Wiley.

and the aptitude for it. The decision to pivot into business was painful, but it was also freeing and, ultimately, far more fruitful.

### *2. Redefine failure as a learning process.*

If life gives you lemons, make lemonade. Trying to avoid failure at all costs leads to stagnation. History shows us that failure is often a stepping stone to victory. Those who embrace their setbacks and learn from them gain wisdom, resilience, and long-term success. Taking calculated risks—even at the cost of short-term losses—is often what separates those who stagnate from those who soar.

### *3. Act ethically, even when it hurts.*

True success is not measured by temporary wins but by enduring character. Ethical choices may cost you in the short run—financially, relationally, or professionally—but they are the foundation for a lasting legacy. As Peter Drucker noted, ethics in business isn't optional; it's essential.[32] Those who are willing to lose opportunities rather than compromise their integrity ultimately gain things far more valuable: trust, credibility, and peace of mind.

---

*You can't go back and make a new start, but you can start right now.*

---

### *4. Surround yourself with people who share your values.*

The people around us shape who we become. If we want to live with creative courage and moral clarity, we must walk with those who value the same. As Robert Putnam[33] wrote, the strength of a

---

[32] Drucker, P. F. (1981). What is "business ethics"? *The Public Interest*, (63), 18–36.

[33] Putnam, R. D. (1993). The prosperous community: Social capital and public life. *The American Prospect*, 4(13), 35–42.

community determines the prosperity of its members. Surround yourself with people who know how to lose well, who embrace failure with humility, and who work hard without selling their soul. Their presence will elevate yours.

In closing, the tension between dissatisfaction and creativity is real and powerful. If we embrace loss not as defeat but as discipline and an essential part of the journey, we will find a deeper, richer kind of contentment—a contentment that creates, leads, adapts, and perseveres.

True fulfillment isn't the absence of failure; it's the presence of peace, even when we fall short. It is found not in conquering every mountain but in trusting the One who moves them.

## Reflection and Discussion

*1. Where do I see this strength—and its shadow—in my own life?*

*2. What situations most often trigger the temptation connected to this strength?*

*3. What safeguards or disciplines can I put in place to cultivate the strength while resisting its temptation?*

*4. Who in my life models this strength well, and what can I learn from their example?*

## Further Reading

Christensen, C. M. (1997). *The innovator's dilemma: When new technologies cause great firms to fail*. Harvard Business School Press.

Donders, P. Ch. (2000). *Kreative Lebensplanung* [Creative life planning]. Gerth Medien GmbH. *(Note: This book is in German; an English edition may not be available.)*

Fukuyama, F. (2014). *Political order and political decay: From the industrial revolution to the globalization of democracy*. Farrar, Straus, and Giroux.

Gibson, R. (2015). *The four lenses of innovation: A power tool for creative thinking*. Wiley.

Gladwell, M. (2013). *David and Goliath: Underdogs, misfits, and the art of battling giants*. Little, Brown and Company.

Heath, C., & Heath, D. (2007). *Made to stick: Why some ideas survive and others die*. Random House.

Maxwell, J. C. (2013). *Sometimes you win, sometimes you learn: Life's greatest lessons are gained from our losses*. Center Street.

Michalowicz, M. (2021). *Get different: Marketing that can't be ignored*. Portfolio.

Miller, D., & Peterson, J. J. (2020). *Marketing made simple: A step-by-step StoryBrand guide for any business*. HarperCollins Leadership.

Pink, D. H. (2009). *Drive: The surprising truth about what motivates us*. Riverhead Books.

Rubin, R. (2023). *The creative act: A way of being*. Penguin Press.

# 5

# DETERMINATION VS. ANGER

THE FIFTH TRAIT I HAVE OBSERVED IN SUCCESSFUL people is *determination*. These individuals exhibit a constructive stubbornness that prevents them from being defeated by life's challenges or discouraged by others' opinions. When they fail, they possess an extraordinary willpower that helps them rebound and not let temporary setbacks define them. In this chapter, we will explore what determination means, how it manifests in our lives and work, and how it contributes to success. Determination can be cultivated through awareness and sustained effort.

However, determined people are also susceptible to temptations that can undermine the benefits of this trait—foremost among them is anger. Why are determined individuals especially prone to anger? What are the consequences of anger? Is it dangerous for someone striving for success? Can anger be neutralized so we can enjoy the benefits of determination without paying the emotional and relational cost? Many of us wrongly believe that anger is uncontrollable. In this chapter, we will examine how to cultivate determination and then turn to the dangers of anger and strategies for curbing it.

## What Is Determination?

"How much you pay for Cotton?" is the question that sparks one of the most memorable bargaining scenes in a Western movie. Mattie

Ross, a 14-year-old girl, embarks on a journey to avenge her father's death. She boldly enters the office of Colonel Stonehill, a merchant from whom her father had purchased a horse, and demands the return of $325. After a tense exchange, young Mattie walks away with exactly what she came for. Though her odds were slim, she stood firm, fought for what she believed was hers, and ultimately succeeded. The movie is *True Grit*, a title which can be understood as "strength of character" and "determination." Mattie's fierce resolve in that negotiation reflects a deep sense of purpose and unwavering self-belief.

I've seen this same trait in successful people.[34] They know what they want from life or from a particular situation. They express their goals and desires simply, clearly, and persuasively. In contrast, people of mediocrity often don't know what they want from life. Even when they do ask for something, they come across as timid, unsure, or awkward. Their requests sound like, "Do you have a glass of water, because I'm so hungry that I don't have a place to sleep," or "I'm so broke I can't even afford to pay attention." In contrast, the determined person asks for water, food, and shelter clearly and directly. I invite you to keep Mattie's gritty attitude in mind as we explore this chapter.

### *1. Determination may be a natural endowment, but it can also be nurtured.*

Some people are born into families with a strong work ethic, well-defined goals, and a clear understanding of the effort required to achieve them. They grow up with positive examples and are shaped by the diligence of their parents.

Others grow up in environments where giving up in the face of adversity is the norm. Sadly, many people use their difficult

---

[34] Duckworth, A. L., & Gross, J. J. (2014). Self-control and grit: Related but separable determinants of success. *Current Directions in Psychological Science, 23*(5), 319–325. https://doi.org/10.1177/0963721414541462.

upbringing or negative role models as lifelong excuses for complacency and lack of resolve. But willpower is one of the most transformative tools God has given us; it can shape all other habits. No matter what we inherit or experience, our will can mobilize us to act.

A person can blame their parents until the age of 14. After that, the reality of one's life becomes largely their own responsibility. I'm not saying that family or genetic gifts don't matter, but ultimately, determination is a choice we must make for ourselves.

### *2. Determination involves accepting rejection and failure.*

Many of us unconsciously desire a life free from these hardships. We fantasize about a perfect world where we are universally accepted, effortlessly successful, and reciprocated in love. But life isn't a movie. Success requires effort and preparation.

Reality is full of rejection and setbacks. Occasionally, something valuable may come with minimal effort, but even a broken clock is right twice a day. If you spend your life staring at that clock, waiting for those two correct moments, you'll live a disappointed life. Determined people acknowledge this truth. When they fall, they get back up. I love Solomon's wisdom: "For though the righteous fall seven times, they rise again, but the wicked stumble when calamity strikes" (Prov. 24:16). Falling is human. Rising is divine.

### *3. Determination means allowing reason to govern emotion.*

God made us beings with feelings. There's nothing wrong with enjoying pleasure, but modern culture tempts us to expect constant pleasure and avoid pain at all costs. We now have endless access to easy, free, or inexpensive entertainment: YouTube, TikTok, Instagram, etc. As a result, we've become conditioned to avoid anything that's boring or demanding. Determination is the force that compels us to prioritize purpose and character over fleeting emotions.

*To fail is human; to rise is divine.*

### *4. Determination should resist despite present realities.*

Successful people can imagine a better world and work tirelessly to create it. In the late 18th century, a group of young American thinkers and leaders—many of whom had studied law, philosophy, and governance in Europe—returned or emerged with a bold vision: an independent and unified United States. At that time, the 13 colonies were loosely connected, largely agrarian, and under British rule. Many around Jefferson, Hamilton, Washington, Madison, and Adams considered their ideas of independence unrealistic or even dangerous. Yet this generation—shaped by their ideals and determined to forge a new kind of nation—led the American Revolution, drafted the Declaration of Independence in 1776, and created a constitution that still governs the country today. Much of what Americans enjoy in terms of democracy, freedom, and national identity can be traced back to the vision and resolve of these extraordinary founders.

Yet determination must be guided by discernment and a sense of divine calling. There's a fine line between perseverance and foolish stubbornness. Wise counsel from people of character can help us discern the difference. Reinhold Niebuhr's famous prayer captures this well: "Lord, grant me the serenity to accept the things I cannot change, courage to change the things I can, and the wisdom to know the difference."[35]

### *5. Determination fights through fatigue and disappointment.*

It's the extra push when you're tired but still need to meet a deadline or reach a goal. As discussed in the previous chapter, successful people manage their time and energy wisely. They monitor what

[35] Niebuhr, R. (1943). *Serenity Prayer.*

motivates or drains them and act proactively. Schwartz and McCarthy stress the importance of understanding one's biorhythm:

> First of all, [people] need to become more aware of how they feel at different times of the working day and the impact these emotions have on their effectiveness. Most people realize that they tend to perform at their best when they feel positive energy.[36]

I recommend tracking your most productive hours for different types of tasks. Writers, for example, may do their best work in the early morning or late at night. By managing their energy, they also manage their time more effectively.

### *6. Determination includes resilience, the ability to recover from defeat.*

Our expectations are key. If we expect only victories, we will be disappointed. Murphy's Law reminds us that "anything that can go wrong will go wrong—at the worst possible time." The real question is not whether we will fall but how we will respond.

During my childhood in America, I came to appreciate American football. As a boy, I admired the players' strength. As a business student, I admired their paychecks. I once watched a documentary that calculated how much football players earned per yard—and even per fall. It made me think life is like football. You're going to get knocked down. The only question is will you get up and keep running or stay down and shout at the referee for the rest of your life?

---

[36] Schwartz, T., & McCarthy, C. (2007). Manage your energy, not your time. *Harvard Business Review*, 85(10), 62–71.

### *7. Determination means rejecting self-pity.*

Self-pity usually begins with a real wound: abuse, injustice, or neglect. Life contains unfathomable suffering. The issue isn't whether our pain is real but whether self-pity helps. It doesn't. Successful people persevere without feeling sorry for themselves. They've learned that a victim mentality solves nothing. Self-pity drains your energy, demotivates you, and repels others. People who wallow in self-pity risk becoming insufferable.

## How Does Determination Manifest Itself?

From my research and experience, determination is rooted in a rational worldview,[37] the belief that life has purpose and actions have consequences. I call this belief *creationism,* not in a narrow theological sense but as a rational principle. If I see a turtle on a post, someone put it there. If I see a well-kept garden, someone maintained it. If I meet a successful person, I assume hard work and discipline are behind it.

Likewise, a chaotic life usually reflects neglect. Sadly, many prefer superstition over logic. Too often, we treat failure like it's a curse, something mysterious or fated. But successful people don't stop there. They ask questions, test assumptions, and try again. Think of the Wright Brothers. When their early flying machines failed, they didn't blame the wind or bad luck. They studied birds, built wind tunnels, and reworked their designs. It was that commitment to learning—not magical thinking—that eventually got them off the ground.

[37] Deci, E. L., & Ryan, R. M. (2012). Self-determination theory. In P. A. Van Lange, A. W. Kruglanski, & E. T. Higgins (Eds.), *Handbook of theories of social psychology* (Vol. 1, pp. 416–436). Sage Publications Ltd.

---

*The time and energy spent on self-pity will demotivate you and will alienate the good people around you.*

---

## The Four Manifestations of Determination

### *1. Determination is decisiveness.*

The U.S. military has a principle that "a wrong decision is better than no decision." Indecisiveness drains energy and creates inertia. Determined people analyze risks but don't get paralyzed by analysis.

### *2. Determination shows up as courage.*

Courage is not the absence of fear but action despite fear. Courage reframes obstacles as growth opportunities. It helps you act boldly and stay the course, seeing failure not as the end but as a step toward success.

### *3. Determination manifests in consistency.*

Like the steady drip of water that shapes stone, small efforts repeated daily yield great results. Fitness coaches say, "Ten minutes a day can change your body." This applies to every area: reading, relationships, work, and more.

### *4. Determination brings focus.*

A wise mentor once told me, "You're like a ray of sunshine—cheerful, warm. But under a magnifying glass, that ray becomes fire. Focused further, it becomes a laser that cuts through steel. What do you want to be?" I want to be that laser—focused, intentional, and effective.

## The Benefits of Determination

Like industriousness, determination doesn't come easy. In the short term, it may not bring immediate rewards. People will doubt you. Dreams will seem distant. But if you approach everything—great or small—with determination, you'll fulfill your responsibilities and eventually see results.

### *1. Determination ensures that you're prepared when opportunity arises.*

As I've written before, success happens when opportunity meets preparation. If you live determinedly, success will find you ready.

### *2. Determination helps you stay the course.*

When you know your destination and believe in your mission, obstacles won't easily deter you. You'll be fueled by purpose and inspired to persevere.

### *3. Determination deepens devotion.*

You'll fulfill your duties in good times and bad. This devotion becomes even more powerful when rooted in altruism—when you understand that your gifts are from God and using them to serve others is your offering of thanks.

### *4. Determination earns trust.*

People will rely on you. You'll be known not just for getting things done but for doing them with integrity and excellence. Your word will carry weight. You will influence others positively. Just as God created the world through words, you also have the power to shape reality through your speech. Successful people understand this and use their words wisely.

## Anger: The Temptation of Determined People

When we face hardship, defeat, or adversity, it is determination that lifts us up and helps us press on. However, I have observed that determined people are particularly vulnerable to the temptation of anger.

The American Psychological Association defines anger as "an emotion characterized by antagonism toward someone or something you feel has deliberately wronged you." This emotion is often strong and sooner or later makes itself visible. At times, anger may even be justified. But justified or not, when anger becomes excessive or uncontrolled, it turns toxic and damages our character, reputation, and even our health. The greatest challenge in managing anger is that it usually feels justified. And precisely because it feels justified, it can fuel outbursts in which we say or do things we later regret. Anger can manifest itself physically, almost uncontrollably. We describe these moments with phrases like "I lost it," "I saw red," or "I was blinded by rage."

Some people are naturally prone to anger. Angry personalities tend to struggle with self-control and react quickly—and sometimes violently—when they feel attacked, wronged, or disrespected. Our upbringing also plays a major role. A person raised in an environment where patience was not valued and emotional outbursts were tolerated is more likely to resort to anger.

Determined people, as we have discussed, are hard-working, goal-oriented, and willing to invest time, energy, and money to reach their objectives. But when their efforts don't produce the expected results—when the law of cause and effect seems broken—anger sets in.

As a professor of entrepreneurship, I'm involved in many startup projects. Students, friends, and collaborators often come to me with business ideas meant to meet a real market need. The process usually begins with analysis and a business plan through which we secure financial and human resources. Then comes implementation, which requires immense amounts of effort, like an airplane revving its engines to overcome gravity. Sadly, even when we do our homework and push to the max, we sometimes fail. Investor money is lost, time is wasted, and our credibility takes a hit. That's when the anger erupts. There is blame and finger-pointing: "Who failed?" "Where did the plan fall short?" "Was the analysis flawed?" "Was the implementation shallow?" "Did our market research lie to us?"

But it's not only entrepreneurs who face failure and frustration; everyone does. Children get angry when their phones or tablets are taken away or when they're forced to eat healthy food. Teenagers get angry when they feel misunderstood or excluded. Students get angry when teachers seem unfair or employers offer unreasonably low wages. Spouses get angry over broken promises and irresponsibility. Citizens are angry when public services fail them, and pensioners feel forgotten after a lifetime of hard work. There's no shortage of situations where anger seems justified.

Some express their anger loudly—shouting, swearing, or using cruel, contemptuous words. Others internalize it—harboring negative thoughts, imagining revenge, or planning avoidance. But anger rarely produces good outcomes. On the contrary, it's often destructive. As St. James wrote, "Human anger does not produce the righteousness that God desires" (Jas. 1:20). At its core, anger springs from a fear of losing control and a sense of helplessness when circumstances fail to meet our expectations.

## How Anger Manifests

### *1. Anger drives impulsive and reckless words and actions—what we might call "jumping the gun."*

Intense emotions cloud our ability to think clearly. We speak or act without considering the consequences, and this can lead to decisions or behaviors we deeply regret. Strong emotions can blind us, leading us to act on instinct rather than reason. In those moments, we might say things to loved ones that they never forget, words that cause long-term harm even if we calm down later. In extreme cases, anger leads to irreversible consequences: quitting a job, breaking a contract, or—in domestic settings—even resorting to violence.

### *2. Anger can manifest through shouting.*

This happens at home and in public places—hospitals, offices, classrooms, and beyond. It's not hard to picture a manager yelling at employees. Shortly after I got married, a new Italian restaurant opened in our town. I took my wife there for an early dinner, hoping for a quiet, romantic meal. Unfortunately, during our meal, the owner—who seemed to be drinking—held a "meeting" in the kitchen. From our table, we could hear shouting and swearing. The waitress tried to maintain a pleasant demeanor, but it was clear she was shaken by the owner's outbursts.

Anger can also appear as self-pity. While determined people typically don't wallow in self-pity, unresolved anger and relational conflict can lead them there. I've met wealthy people with influence who complained they couldn't pay their bills. I've met attractive, talented people who insisted that nobody wanted them and that they had no prospects.

### *3. Anger can be conspiratorial.*

It grows silently beneath the surface until it boils over. When you start believing that everyone and everything is against you, resentment builds. Even if you've been genuinely wronged, feeding your mind only with grievances leads to bitterness. Eventually, the pressure becomes too much, and the anger explodes—often over something trivial. The angry person might say things like these: "I'll handle it myself"; "You don't need to tell me"; "I know who you are"; or "You and your whole kind..."

### *4. Anger shows up through cynicism.*

Cynicism often manifests through words that cut, skepticism that poisons relationships, and a refusal to believe the best in others. Empathy disappears. You assume the worst and justify your own harmful behavior. Cynical people use extreme phrases like "You always," "You never," "There's no point," "There's no one worth talking to," or "I'll just shut up."

### *5. The angry person seeks control.*

When they feel they're losing it—or their position is threatened—they assert themselves through anger. This control becomes oppressive as they attempt to dictate the behavior and thoughts of those around them. Rather than resolving issues through communication and collaboration, they stoke conflict and deepen resentment. I've seen it time and again: parents, teachers, and bosses who lose respect because they try to lead through anger—only to see their influence disappear. Fortunately, many victims of such anger eventually find ways to break free.

### *6. The angry person manipulates.*

The sixth manifestation is manipulation. Determined people trapped by anger often resort to emotional blackmail and coercion. They prey on the ignorance or limited options of those around them. After major U.S. industries moved manufacturing overseas in the late 20th century, a new class of business leaders emerged who capitalized on cheap global labor. Many American workers, especially in the Rust Belt, lost stable jobs and had few alternatives to accept lower-paying, less secure work. When I started speaking out against this model in the early 2000s, some dismissed it as inevitable. But sure enough, when new industries—like tech and logistics—began offering better opportunities in different regions, people left in droves, seeking jobs with fairer pay and better prospects.

## The Effects of Anger

Even if people feel justified in their anger, its effects are rarely constructive.[38] These consequences appear across all areas of life and should motivate us to address our anger, not excuse it.

### *1. Tense Environments*

When anger becomes the default form of communication, every conversation risks becoming a conflict. Instead of resolving problems peacefully, anger escalates them, making lasting solutions harder to reach.

### *2. Loss of Character*

Angry outbursts can destroy the good reputation you've built through years of hard work. People won't remember your determination; they'll remember your impulsive words and actions. The damage will hurt others, but most of all, it will hurt you. My father was a chronically angry man. His anger, combined with drinking, made our childhood difficult. Tragically, he knew what he was doing was harmful. He used to sing an old song repeatedly: "When you become a burden to yourself . . ."—he would sing and cry but not control his anger and drinking.

### *3. Loss of Trust*

Reputations and relationships—carefully built over time—can be ruined by anger. People will avoid you, stop taking your calls, and stop replying to your messages. Sometimes they walk away without giving you a chance to apologize. That silence—that absence—is the most painful consequence of all.

---

[38] Ellis, A., & Tafrate, R. C. (1997). *How to control your anger before it controls you.* Birch Lane Press.

### *4. Hasty, Irrational Decisions*

Anger clouds judgment and compromises your ability to think clearly. Decisions made in a fit of rage—quitting a job, breaking off a relationship, or making a major purchase—often lead to regret. They waste time, money, relationships, and opportunities. And once those are lost, they may never return. Because I, too, struggle with anger, I regularly return to the wisdom of Solomon:

> He who is slow to anger is better than the mighty, and he who rules his spirit than he who takes a city. (Prov. 16:32)

## Heavenly Reward: A Solution for Anger

We've observed two common extremes in people who are driven to succeed but struggle with anger.

---

*He who is slow to anger is better than the mighty, and he who rules his spirit than he who takes a city.*

---

The first group includes those who are naturally determined. They embrace their drive and ambition but accept anger as a necessary byproduct. They see it as the "cost of doing business," even if they're aware of the relational and emotional fallout. Some even shrug it off with phrases such as, "Like it or not, this is just how it is." These individuals often prioritize goals over people, and if forced to choose, they'll abandon relationships—personal or professional—rather than alter their temperament.

The second group is made up of those who are highly self-aware when it comes to their anger. Rather than risk losing control, they retreat. Some step back from leadership roles, decline promotions, or avoid public responsibilities altogether. A few become overly self-punishing, haunted by past mistakes. They might subject themselves to unhealthy work environments or toxic relationships as a form of self-imposed penance.

In this section, I will offer a third way, one grounded in Christian faith. I don't presume to criticize anyone's path. As the Spanish proverb goes, "Each man is an universe." I will share what has helped me and countless others throughout history: a spiritual framework for maintaining resolve and ambition without being consumed by anger.

## The Purpose of Life

According to Christian teaching, this life is preparation for the next. I believe we are eternal souls housed in temporary bodies, and our time on earth—with all its ups and downs—is meant to shape our character for eternity. I believe in a God who is infinite, eternal, and good and who rewards righteousness. I also believe in the existence of a devil, a created being who once was an angel but rebelled against God. The world is the battleground in this cosmic struggle, and each of us chooses daily whose side we're on.

The devil manipulates our broken nature and external circumstances to lure us into destructive cycles: bankruptcy, betrayal, corruption, war, and injustice. His goal is to provoke us, push us toward bitterness and rage, and turn us into agents of evil. God allows trials, not because He enjoys our pain but because they test and reveal our hearts.

I've met many people who claimed to be working for a noble cause—until someone crossed them. Then they exploded. Trials test whether our motives are pure and whether we value people and character more than outcomes and control.

When the Israelites were led out of slavery in Egypt, it took 40 years of wandering in the desert for the slave mentality to be purged. Before entering the Promised Land, Moses reminded them,

> Remember how the Lord your God led you all the way in the wilderness these forty years, to humble and test

> you in order to know what was in your heart, whether or not you would keep his commands. He humbled you, causing you to hunger and then feeding you with manna, which neither you nor your ancestors had known, to teach you that man does not live on bread alone but on every word that comes from the mouth of the Lord. (Deut. 8:2-3)

In the same way, I believe that everyone pursuing success will face a "wilderness" period, a time when we are tested. We ask ourselves in these moments: do we value integrity or results? Do we use people to gain things, or use things to serve people? Every hardship is a chance to show that we value the eternal soul more than the temporary body.

As I wrote at the beginning of this book, the guiding verse of my life is this: "Do not be overcome by evil but overcome evil with good" (Rom. 12:21). That is true success: to be faced with evil and respond with good.

## How Can We Stay Calm in the Storm?

### 1. *Trust that God is in control.*

Knowing that God is sovereign allows me to be at peace, regardless of whether things go right or wrong in business, relationships, or family life. He is both powerful and good, so even if He allows difficulty, it's not meaningless. As Paul writes,

> And we know that in all things God works for the good of those who love him, who have been called according to his purpose. (Rom. 8:28)

When I feel anger rising because something isn't working out, it's usually a sign I've forgotten that I'm not in control or that I've started to rely too much on myself.

---

*Be still.*

---

*2. Remember that you are responsible for effort, not outcomes.*

Farming teaches us this: we plant, water, pull weeds, and build fences—but we cannot force a harvest. Only God can make things grow.

No matter how hard I try, I can't force a client to pay, a student to succeed, or a venture to flourish. Believing otherwise is an illusion and a heavy burden that can easily turn into frustration and anger.

*3. Rest in the truth that God rewards.*

I've studied countless lives, from the Christian tradition and beyond, and I've found that people who believe in divine justice and eternal reward are the ones who live with the most peace. They don't have to explode, manipulate, or control. They can breathe. They can serve. And in the end, they succeed—both in this life and the next.

In the next chapter, we'll explore altruism and the temptation of betrayal.

## Reflection and Discussion

*1. Where do I see this strength—and its shadow—in my own life?*

*2. What situations most often trigger the temptation connected to this strength?*

*3. What safeguards or disciplines can I put in place to cultivate the strength while resisting its temptation?*

*4. Who in my life models this strength well, and what can I learn from their example?*

# Further Reading

Arnold, C. L. (2013). *Small steps, big changes: A breakthrough program to transform your life with a single action*. Wiley.

Eker, H. T. (2005). *Secrets of the millionaire mind: Mastering the inner game of wealth*. Harper Business.

Elmore, T. (2019). *The 8 paradoxes of great leaders: How to always have the answers to today's contradictory demands at hand*. Thomas Nelson.

Godin, S. (2007). *The dip: A little book that teaches when to quit (and when to persevere)*. Penguin.

Johnson, S. (1992). *Yes or no: A guide to effective decision-making*. Doubleday.

Mauborgne, R., & Kim, W. C. (2005). *Blue ocean strategy: How to create uncontested market space and make the competition irrelevant*. Harvard Business Review Press.

Maxwell, J. C. (2007). *The 21 indispensable laws of leadership: Follow them and people will follow you*. Thomas Nelson.

Metaxas, E. (2013). *Seven men and their secrets*. Thomas Nelson.

Robertson, I. (2017). *The secrets of self-confidence*. HarperCollins.

Sinek, S. (2009). *Start with why: How great leaders inspire everyone to take action*. Portfolio.

Wickman, G. (2017). *Traction: Get a grip on your business*. BenBella Books.

Ziglar, Z. (2001). *Objectives: How to get more*. Thomas Nelson.

---

*Dream big, work hard, stay focused, and surround yourself with good people.*

---

# 6

# ALTRUISM VS. REVENGE

THE SIXTH TRAIT I HAVE OBSERVED AMONG SUCCESSFUL people is *altruism*. Unfortunately, a widespread misconception—fueled by classic literature, the media, and Hollywood—portrays the wealthy as stingy, greedy, and corrupt. A classic example is Scrooge, the famous British character created by Charles Dickens, a cruel, miserly, rich man who exploits others. I am not saying that rich people are unselfish; I am saying that successful people are unselfish. As we've already established, successful people are sometimes wealthy, but not all wealthy people are truly successful. Based on my research and experience, altruism is a defining trait that often distinguishes the merely rich from the genuinely successful.

Because altruism is often misunderstood—or understood differently than how I define it—I want to begin by clarifying what I mean by the term. For our purposes, altruism is a general attitude successful people have toward money and material resources. That's the perspective from which we'll explore this topic. Later, we'll examine revenge, the specific temptation that often haunts altruistic individuals. Finally, I'll offer a few practical solutions for cultivating genuine altruism while resisting the lure of revenge, which, as we will see, can be deeply destructive.

---

*Earn as much as you can,*
*Save as much as you can,*
*Give as much as you can!*

---

## What Is Altruism?

Whenever I speak about this concept,[39] especially to those outside the business world, people often light up. Many times, someone will say to me, "Professor, tell those rich people to be more generous—just look at how much we need! They've got more money than they know what to do with." I've met individuals with little material wealth who carry an attitude of entitlement. Not a week goes by without a request from a struggling family or an urgent case in need of financial help.

Of course, I support generosity. But I've also seen well-intentioned generosity lead to dependence, laziness, and manipulation. That's why I believe altruism is more than just generosity. Altruism is the mindset of a wise investor, captured in the Protestant work ethic from the 16th and 17th centuries and in this admonition from John Wesley: "Earn as much as you can, save as much as you can, and give as much as you can."

## The Four Components of Altruism

### *1. Understanding of Accounting*

A common trait of mediocre people is a lack of financial tracking. They may know their income, but they seldom monitor their expenses. For some, financial management is a mystery they never attempt to solve. I've worked with clients and students who felt their income was insufficient—until I asked them to record their monthly spending. Only then did they realize where their money was going. You cannot manage what you don't measure. Successful people recognize that time and money are their two most powerful tools, and they have systems in place to monitor and manage both with precision.

---

[39] Graham, B., & McGowan, B. (2003). *The intelligent investor*. Harper Business Essentials.

### *2. Understanding of Finance*

While accounting tracks the past, finance forecasts the future. Successful individuals don't just talk about goals and dreams; they plan for them. They understand the nature of investments, the cost of debt, and the value of return. One of my favorite principles is, "Hardworking people have even harder-working money." Their investments work while they sleep or take time off. Consider this example:

> $1.00 saved and left alone for a year stays $1.00.
> $1.01 compounded daily for a year becomes $37.78.

That's the power of small, consistent effort and the wisdom of long-term thinking.

### *3. A Win-Win Mentality*

Successful people certainly care about growing their income and influence, but they also think long-term. They are constantly seeking a balance between personal gain and communal benefit. In business, they understand the importance of meeting the needs of employees, clients, suppliers, and the government. They work tirelessly to keep that ecosystem in harmony.

### *4. True Generosity*

Misapplied generosity can cause tension, broken relationships, and even foster the temptation of revenge. Many people view generosity only in financial terms and practice it either out of guilt or from a sense of superiority.

While American culture is often associated with a strong entrepreneurial spirit and a focus on financial literacy, it's still common to find individuals who prioritize short-term gains over long-term investments. However, I've encountered many altruistic individuals who, despite the challenges they face, recognize the importance of investing for the future. They understand that if you want to reap the rewards tomorrow, you have to sow the seeds today—whether it's through time, money, or effort. This mindset aligns with the American ethos of self-reliance and the belief that success requires patience and strategic planning. Whatever field you're in, without a healthy dose of altruism, you will not succeed. If you're not willing to sacrifice short-term comfort to invest in long-term growth, your future will never be better than your present.

## What Does Altruism Look Like?

What does an altruistic person actually look like, someone willing to make sacrifices and take risks?

### 1. *They are helpful.*

They tend to say "yes" when asked for help. Need support with a project? They'll try their best. In crisis? They're the ones who'll say, "I've got your back." They offer time, mentorship, jobs, and even loans when needed.

### 2. *They are often sociable.*

If the altruist is also an extrovert, they tend to be the life of the party. They lift others with humor, create atmosphere, and make people feel seen. Their charisma and openness attract incredible people and opportunities. People gravitate to them, saying things like "I want to work with you," "Let's partner up," and "Can I get your advice?" Their willingness to help creates a magnetic kind of influence.

Though it may seem counterintuitive, altruism draws success. Consider Warren Buffett, one of the most admired investors of all time. His generosity in offering free, insightful advice earned him the nickname "The Oracle of Omaha." That generosity also drew powerful connections and continuous opportunities.

### *3. They are family-oriented and community-minded.*

They don't walk away from those closest to them. In fact, they go out of their way to support and elevate those around them. This archetype is captured, surprisingly, in the character of Don Corleone from *The Godfather*. As an Italian immigrant facing the hardships of a new life in America, he helped his family, neighbors, and community. He found them jobs, negotiated their rent, and even arranged marriages. Whatever problem the Italian immigrant community faced, Don Corleone and his team would solve it. Those who benefited from his help became part of the *Cosa Nostra* and, in return, received protection.

### *4. They know how to barter.*

Successful individuals are highly strategic. They know how to trade something small on their end—like a phone call or a word of recommendation—for something incredibly valuable to someone else: a job, lower rent, or early access to a program. Yes, that favor usually comes with an unspoken obligation. Does this make them manipulative? Not necessarily. The exchange of favors can be productive, healthy, and even necessary—but it can also invite tension, unmet expectations, and complicated dynamics.

## The Benefits of Altruism

In his book *The Tipping Point: How Little Things Can Make a Big Difference,*[40] Malcolm Gladwell introduces the concept of "mavens," individuals who excel at weaving relationships, connecting people, and creating ecosystems. This exemplifies one aspect of altruism.

---

[40] Gladwell, M. (2006). *The tipping point: How little things can make a big difference.* Little, Brown.

### *1. Altruism is beneficial on a personal level.*

An altruist can attest that every good deed, piece of advice, act of financial support, or kind word brings a sense of well-being, energy, and joy. Altruism is a source of almost limitless internal power. It's not uncommon to hear of people who work long hours, travel extensively, and endure many inconveniences who are driven by the desire to do good and help others.

The benefits of altruism extend beyond the individual.

### *2. Altruism makes a profound impact on those around us.*

Selfless people have the power to transform lives. Some open doors for others by sharing the resources they have at their disposal. Others offer their knowledge or perhaps the most valuable resource of all: time. Looking back, altruists find fulfillment in knowing that someone's life was changed because of them—that someone found a job, met their life partner, or simply got through a difficult time because someone stood by them.

The beauty of altruism is that every person who is helped, changed, or empowered is, in turn, positioned to help, change, and empower others.

### *3. Altruism changes society.*

A compelling example of this is fundraising for social causes such as education or supporting people with disabilities. It often begins with one individual, a visionary with enthusiasm and, ideally, connections. This person commits to a cause, and their passion becomes contagious. For the campaign to succeed, the visionary must engage two or three key donors (i.e., "anchor donors") whose influence and resources help spread the message and draw in additional supporters. As the movement grows, fundraising flourishes, people feel fulfilled, and society benefits from the collective contribution. In this way, an altruistic vision touches lives, and each of those lives touches others. Piece by piece, the world becomes a better place.

Perhaps one of the most remarkable examples of this is Bill Gates. Beyond his philanthropic efforts, the greatest contribution of this successful individual is the inspiration he has sparked in an entire generation of millionaires, motivating them to become philanthropists themselves. Gates has shown us the power of an altruistic individual to mobilize and inspire, even to the point of making altruism contagious.

## Revenge: The Temptation of the Altruist

After such a description, one might almost think that altruists are saints, perfect individuals who always do good and never get angry.[41] But we know that such people do not exist, and every positive trait of successful individuals brings with it at least one temptation they must resist. In the case of altruism, the great temptation is revenge in response to betrayal.

*A successful person is very likely to be betrayed.*

Selfless people, by definition, are open to betrayal. They are those willing to help, hire, and invest. They often do more than is asked of them and sometimes even take on tasks that haven't been requested. They interact with others in good faith and have a legitimate expectation of appreciation, if not reward. Unfortunately, there's an old saying that captures a harsh truth: "No good deed goes unpunished." This speaks to the idea that sometimes even when you act selflessly or help others, you can be taken advantage of or betrayed in return.

[41] Beattie, H. J. (2005). Revenge. *Journal of the American Psychoanalytic Association, 53*(2), 513–524. https://doi.org/10.1177/00030651050530020601.

Most can relate to betrayal and the pain of unacknowledged effort. Think about business leaders like Steve Jobs, who, after being ousted from Apple—the company he founded—used that betrayal as fuel to create NeXT and Pixar, eventually returning to Apple and transforming it into one of the most valuable companies in the world.

A harsh reality, whether in business or personal life, is that our best efforts to help or uplift others are sometimes met with disappointment or betrayal. This reality is often reflected in the stories of famous leaders, philanthropists, or entrepreneurs who were betrayed by those they trusted, yet they persevered and grew stronger from the experience. When you act with the best intentions—whether by helping someone in need or supporting a cause—sometimes the return is not gratitude but betrayal or envy. Just like those who rose above their setbacks, the key is not to let betrayal define you. Instead, it's about enduring and finding strength through it.

Another significant issue faced by altruistic, successful individuals is competition. In Western cultures, competition is often viewed as a motivator, fueling people to grow, prosper, and become successful. When someone succeeds, the typical Western reaction is, "*If he can do it, so can I. What makes him special? What can he do that I can't?*" Competition drives them to improve themselves and outdo the successful individual by legitimate means. In this context, competition can be constructive, propelling development and progress. However, competition resulting from envy can be incredibly destructive.

A group of three men was captured by cannibals. Before their execution, the captors granted them one weekend to do whatever they wished. The first man decided he would return home, enjoy a comfortable chair, and read his favorite books. The second one chose to spend the entire weekend in a wine cellar. The third man, however, looked at the others and said, "I'm going back to my village to burn down the house of the man I envy." This anecdote reflects the destructive nature of envy, where satisfaction is sometimes derived from the failure of others.

Faced with these harsh realities, I have encountered individuals who have either abandoned altruism or suppressed it in favor of revenge.

## What Does Revenge Look Like?

Sadly, many successful people who experience betrayal or envy no longer act; they react.[42] After all you've done for others and after all the hard work and sacrifice, is this the payoff? No problem. You'll show them you can be different! Did they stab you in the back? No problem. You'll prove who has more venom and a sharper sword! Unfortunately, when a person reacts in this way, they channel all their energy into revenge, nullifying their own ability to progress.

## The Seven Facets of Revenge

### *1. Revenge is linked to indebtedness.*

Every act of help is meticulously accounted for and evaluated. The most vulnerable individuals are those backed into a corner, lacking money and alternatives. The generous person may turn into a manipulator, always ensuring that others owe him something. Nothing is truly free; any altruistic action is followed by an unspoken expectation that will be revealed when the recipient least expects it.

### *2. Revenge can arise from a desire for respect.*

Revenge wears many guises, and one of them is the expectation of respect. This manifestation of manipulation works as follows. The investor expects to be treated with extreme deference, perhaps even receiving admiration or loyalty. A person may offer help or

---

[42] Porath, C., & Pearson, C. (2013). The price of incivility. *Harvard Business Review, 91*(1-2), 114–121.

investment, but the price demanded is respect, often intertwined with loyalty and obedience. Returning to the example of Don Corleone in *The Godfather*, "respect" is his favorite word, and he is willing to go to great lengths—such as killing someone—to get the respect he believes he is due.

### *3. Revenge can be linked to a pathological need for applause.*

The need for respect can escalate, and the person seeking revenge may come to believe that she deserves recognition for everything she has done. She craves praise and publicity. In other words, those who have benefited from her generosity must constantly applaud her, publicly acknowledging the sacrifices made. She wants everyone to know how difficult the situation would have been without her intervention and how lucky the recipient was to have been rescued.

### *4. Revenge is linked to envy.*

The individual who seeks revenge often falls prey to envy as well. After experiencing betrayal, he may begin to compare himself to others, especially those who seem to thrive without facing the same setbacks. Envy takes root, shifting his focus from personal achievements to a fixation on others' success. This leads to regrets and resentment: "I'm sorry I helped him." "I shouldn't have gotten involved with him." "Who made me get involved?"

### *5. Revenge is based on insecurity.*

Comparison breeds resentment, and those caught in this cycle often disparage others' accomplishments instead of using them as inspiration. This destructive cycle deepens their sense of inadequacy, driving them further away from their own path and potential success.

### *6. Revenge creates compromise.*

When consumed by betrayal and envy, individuals may become desperate to regain success at any cost. This desperation leads to dangerous compromises as the lust for revenge clouds their judgment. Integrity, values, and principles may be discarded in pursuit of quick fixes or validation. Instead of focusing on sustainable progress, they resort to unethical decisions or manipulative tactics, ultimately eroding their character and pushing them further away from true success.

### *7. Revenge can be passive.*

Revenge can manifest as inactivity or passivity taken to the extreme. Individuals trapped by betrayal, resentment, and conspiracy theories can become paralyzed by frustration. They may deliberately sabotage projects or institutions. I've encountered cases where individuals retaliated by failing to do what they promised or should have done. Their inaction was a form of revenge, one that harmed the team or client in the process.

## The Dangers of Revenge

As the mindset and practice of revenge grow,[43] the formerly successful and altruistic individual begins to fall deeper into paranoia, convinced that others are plotting against him. New collaborators pay for the mistakes of old ones, and trust disappears. The presumption of guilt prevails in every relationship, transforming everything into an economic and relational barter.

I once spoke at a conference where I emphasized the importance of optimism and the dangers of pessimism. During a break, someone

[43] Goleman, D., Boyatzis, R. E., Boyatzis, R. E., McKee, A., & Finkelstein, S. (2017). *Everyday emotional intelligence: Big ideas and practical advice on how to be human at work*. Harvard Business Press.

approached me and said, "Professor, do you know what a pessimist is? It's an experienced optimist. If you still believe in optimism, you haven't lived long enough." How tragic it is that there are people, scarred by betrayal, who no longer want to help others, no longer want to build, and even enter into the circle of evil. Betrayed people, in turn, betray others.

Revenge can warp a successful person's view of the world, turning them into someone who sees everyone else as an enemy. It magnifies failures. Every challenge, disagreement, or obstacle becomes part of a grand conspiracy designed to undermine their success. In their mind, former allies transform into hidden enemies, and the successes of others are viewed as deliberate attempts to overshadow them. This mindset clouds their ability to recognize support or goodwill, further isolating them.

Historically, we have seen what revenge between nations can mean. Take the Middle East, where Jews and Arabs, fueled by centuries-old grievances, feel the need to avenge wrongs committed thousands of years ago. We also have the tragic example of the former Yugoslavia, where revenge in the name of war led to unimaginable atrocities.

I've observed that the easiest way to stop good and disrupt progress is to take a mistake—whether made willfully or carelessly—and let it roll down the generations, creating a vicious cycle of revenge. Policies pay the price, generation after generation. If you cannot overcome evil with good, you may find yourself becoming part of this circle of evil.

---

*Forgiveness is the sweetest revenge.*
*— Isaac Friedmann*

---

## Divine Vengeance: A Solution Against Revenge

As we have seen, there is a temptation for successful altruists who have been betrayed. They either fall into the circle of evil and seek revenge or isolate themselves and do nothing. Based on my Christian faith, I believe there is a third way: divine vengeance. This means leaving vengeance in God's hands and continuing on the path of selflessness and success, having learned the lesson.

I'll begin this section with a quote from St. Paul, who has helped me—and countless others—overcome the pain of betrayal:

> Return to no one evil for evil. Follow what is right before all men. If it is possible, as much as it depends on you, live peaceably with all men. Dearly beloved, avenge not yourselves, but rather give place unto wrath: for it is written, "Vengeance is mine; I will repay," says the Lord. Therefore if your enemy is hungry, feed him; if he is thirsty, give him drink; for in doing so, you will heap coals of fire on his head. Do not be overcome by evil, but overcome evil with good." (Rom. 12:17-21)

The natural question is, "Where does betrayal come from?" This is, of course, a deep and philosophical question, one that falls into the category of asking, "What is the source of evil in the world?" In simple terms, I believe betrayal comes from human nature, which is prone to selfishness and a lack of empathy. Most betrayals are circumstantial, justified by the context. While many acts of betrayal seem premeditated, they are often the result of haste, superficial judgment, and self-justification.

This does not mean the traitor is innocent. It does not mean that betrayal does not hurt or come at a cost. I've witnessed profitable, valuable businesses destroyed overnight by betrayal. I had a client who, upon discovering that his business partner had embezzled the company's financial reserves, suffered a heart attack and was rushed to the hospital. I do not wish to minimize the pain that betrayal causes; it is one of the most devastating experiences a person can face, especially when it comes from those closest to them.

But I believe that betrayal is allowed in our lives as a testing or purifying tool. As we've been discussing altruism, I think you've seen how easily an altruist can be overtaken by hypocrisy and selfishness. Altruism can morph into self-serving actions, done for the sake of public image or out of a hidden desire to manipulate others or boast. Don Corleone, for example, was not an altruistic magnate but a notorious gangster who would offer favors and kill someone for not remaining loyal.

I see betrayal in a person's life as a test of motivation. Altruism must be purified through betrayal to prove its sincerity. Without this trial, a person may not be altruistic at all but merely a good trader, offering gifts without openly stating the terms of the bargain. God allows these painful experiences to test where our hearts truly lie.

Barter relationships—those unconscious exchanges of good deeds with an expectation of return—often break down when, instead of gratitude, we receive malice, betrayal, or mockery. The temptation is to build protective walls around ourselves and alienate others. This isolation can deeply affect successful people, causing them to become loners who have lost trust in others. And it can happen even in family relationships where betrayal is often more painful.

Betrayal in the family can arise in many painful forms: conflicts over inheritance, family businesses, or land—situations where one person feels the sting of betrayal after investing years of work and sacrifice.

In the face of betrayal and injustice, there is a higher solution than revenge or retreat: trusting in God's retribution.

Parents who have sacrificed their youth for the good of their children experience a devastating betrayal when a child, having benefited from their sacrifices, refuses to work in the family business or asks for their inheritance too early, seeking independence. This was the case in Jesus' Parable of the Prodigal Son. Betrayal and disappointment often come at a high cost.

Despite the pain, God tolerates betrayal not as punishment but as a divine test. The central question of this test is, "From whom do you expect reward?" Do you do good to gain gratitude from men, or do you do good out of love for God, expecting reward from Him? Based on my observations and research, this detached attitude toward results is a tremendous advantage for people who find long-term success. Their responsibility is to plant or water, and they delegate the responsibility for growth and results to God. This process purifies motivations, leading to stronger faith and greater peace.

In the face of betrayal and injustice, the real solution is not rebellion or retreat but trusting in God's reward. It's natural to expect gratitude or loyalty when you invest time, effort, or resources in others. However, the true test of faith is to base your expectations not on the reactions of others but on God's divine promises. I have experienced this divine reward countless times and witnessed it in the lives of many successful people. Someone you've helped betrays you, but then someone you've never met, who you haven't even shared a cup of coffee with, does something extraordinary for you that changes the course of your life.

This experience teaches me to pray to our Father in heaven, not to anyone in earthly positions of power. My reward comes from heaven, not from men. As it is written, "Cursed is the man who trusts in man!" (Jer. 17:5).

The true test of faith is to base your expectations not on the reactions and rewards of others but on the divine promise of God's justice and provision.

---

*In the face of betrayal and injustice, there is a higher solution than revenge or retaliation: waiting for God's retribution.*

---

Betrayal is a trial of faith, a test that scrutinizes our motives and gives us the opportunity to show that our values are built not on human reciprocity but on trust in heavenly reward. This mindset protects us from both the suffering caused by disappointment in people and the temptation to isolate ourselves. The solution is neither to close yourself off nor to expect betrayal to never happen again; instead, it's to trust in God, the only source of true justice. His reward is not temporary, nor is it conditional on the actions or loyalty of others. It comes according to your faith and steadfastness in good. That is why I love the psalmist's words:

> Whom have I in heaven but Thee? And on earth, I desire nothing besides Thee. (Ps. 73:25)

Therefore, when you are betrayed or wronged, the real gain does not come from seeking what you think you deserve from people but from trusting that God will be your portion and inheritance. Only in this way can you overcome the pain of betrayal and the temptation to see yourself as a victim while preserving your integrity and peace of mind.

## Just Revenge

I believe that divine vengeance offers a better alternative to human vengeance because humans are inherently subjective. We suffer from betrayal, but that betrayal may be imagined or based on unrealistic expectations.

The year I started teaching at Emanuel University, a group of high school students was invited to sit in on one of my lectures. One of the more outspoken students, perhaps trying to joke around, said, "Professor, this course was so great I think you should get a percentage of the salary of all the students you've taught." Now, imagine if, in my frustration or pride, I had actually entertained this ridiculous notion. As someone with old-school values, I would never have communicated such an expectation to the students, leaving them no room to correct me. But I might have convinced myself that, if they were truly people of integrity, they should just know who made their success possible. How absurd would it be if I, based on this childish thought, decided to retaliate against students who didn't give me a cut of their earnings? Sadly, I've witnessed many instances where unreasonable and unrealistic expectations have led to destructive acts of revenge.

Another example can be seen in the relationship between parents and children. Parents may offer financial support instead of a bank loan, thus creating an unspoken "social interest." Parents show their generosity by helping their children buy a home, but this act often comes with tacit expectations. For example, parents might feel entitled to criticize their children's life decisions, creating a cycle of manipulation and resentment. It's a clear example of how family relationships can become chains of unhealthy obligations, ultimately causing a sense of betrayal for both parents and children.

## Defense, Not Revenge

This section may be the most controversial in the whole book, so consider yourself forewarned! I have observed that some people prefer revenge to defense. We often hear the phrase, "Don't get mad; get even." This sentiment[44] suggests vengeance is the natural response when we've been wronged. In this mindset, many people choose to seek revenge rather than simply defend themselves. An example of this can be seen in stories of corporate betrayal, like those of high-profile business figures who've been backstabbed by colleagues or partners. Instead of focusing on protecting their interests and moving forward, they might become consumed with the idea of retaliation, either trying to ruin the careers of those who wronged them or engaging in public feuds. This cycle of vengeance can be damaging not only to those involved but also to one's own peace of mind and success. While standing up for oneself is important, it's essential to remember that defense doesn't require revenge. True success lies in responding to conflict with strength, not bitterness. On the other hand, there are people who believe that being victimized gives them a sense of superiority through a type of perceived spiritual and moral purity. This can be just as damaging.

---

[44] Cloud, H. (2023). *Trust: Knowing when to give it, when to withhold it, how to earn it, and how to fix it when it gets broken*. Worthy Publishing.

Perhaps this sounds a bit harsh, but I've found that the most painful price of success is letting go of unhealthy but comfortable relationships. We have people in our lives—whether from childhood or family—with whom it is incredibly hard to part ways. Even worse, there are people who have betrayed us and harmed others, and we don't know how to defend ourselves. Somehow, we think things will be different for us. As the saying goes, "Fool me once, shame on you. Fool me twice, shame on me."[45] There is a fundamental difference between forgiveness and restoration. Forgiveness is mandatory and done for our own peace. Restoration, on the other hand, is optional and based on earned trust.

## Forgiveness and Restoration

When I refuse to forgive, it's like drinking a cup of poison and expecting the person next to me to die. Unforgiveness is the poison that can kill our souls. Forgiveness is a matter of the will and has nothing to do with one's feelings or with apologizing to the wrongdoer. Letting go of the burden of revenge is the central principle of Christian forgiveness.

However, forgiveness does not necessarily mean restoring the relationship. It's perfectly natural and Christian to forgive someone but still choose *not* to work with the person. In many cases, such restoration would likely result in further manipulation and betrayal in the future. Restoration must happen naturally, based on the fruits of change.

Moreover, the betrayer is not excused. Betrayal driven by envy, malice, or a lack of character is never justified. Their actions remain reprehensible. But it is equally important to realize that it is not our job to punish betrayal. Attempts to retaliate, to respond to evil with evil, only lead us further away from goodness. Personal retaliation may seem like a satisfactory short-term solution, but its long-term

---

[45] Weldon, A. (1651). *The court and character of King James*. Printed by R.I., sold by J. Collins.

consequences are devastating for both the perpetrator and those around them. When you are betrayed, it is essential to maintain your moral integrity, continue doing good, and leave revenge in God's hands.

Make a clear distinction between forgiveness and restoration. Forgiving a betrayal does not mean you must accept being betrayed again or maintain the same relationship with the person. Forgiveness is an act of inner liberation, a letting go of the desire for revenge, but restoring the relationship requires trust and a rebuilding of damaged bonds. Sometimes forgiveness may lead to deciding that the relationship cannot continue under the same terms. In our lives, forgiveness must be accompanied by discernment to decide whether the relationship can be restored.

## Pivoting and Development

I have observed that successful people who leave vengeance in God's hands gain the freedom to refocus and pivot. If they choose not to retaliate or wallow in self-pity, they will have the freedom to identify new opportunities. Some people have told me that losing their job was the greatest blessing of their lives. A teenager I met, who had been convicted of drug use, woke up to reality in prison and turned his life around.

Were they shut out of a project? Betrayed by a group? Successful people don't get stuck in front of a closed door; they look for alternatives that often turn out to be far better than the seemingly hopeless situation they faced.

In Silicon Valley, countless betrayals have turned into blessings. People who were betrayed or even ousted from their own companies, like Steve Jobs, have redirected their energies toward new ventures.

This doesn't mean you should seek betrayal or accept negative situations like unemployment. But it does mean that, when you face such challenges, you need to focus on constructive ways to overcome them.

In this chapter, we've introduced altruism as the sixth trait of successful people—what it means, how it manifests, and how we can cultivate it. We've also looked at betrayal, the intrinsic temptation of selfless people, and how we can maintain our altruism through faith in God while redirecting ourselves toward better opportunities.

## Reflection and Discussion

*1. Where do I see this strength—and its shadow—in my own life?*

*2. What situations most often trigger the temptation connected to this strength?*

*3. What safeguards or disciplines can I put in place to cultivate the strength while resisting its temptation?*

*4. Who in my life models this strength well, and what can I learn from their example?*

## Further Reading:

Anderson, C. (2024). *Infectious Generosity: The Supreme Idea Worth Spreading*. W. H. Allen.

Baer, M. R. (2006). *Business as mission: The power of business in the kingdom of God*. YWAM Publishing.

Burg, B., & Mann, J. D. (2016). *The Generous Leader: A Story About What Really Matters in Business*. Simple Truths.

Dayton, H. (2003). *Your Money Matters: A Biblical Guide to Learning How to Spend, Save, Invest, Give, and Get Out of Debt*. Moody Publishers.

Droppers, W. (2021). *The Jerusalem Entrepreneur*. High Bridge Books.

Hill, R. (2013). *Wealth Without Guilt*. Helping Hands Press.

Housel, M. (2020). *The Psychology of Money: Timeless Lessons on Wealth, Greed, and Happiness*. Harriman House.

Jordan-Evans, S., & Beverly, M. (2003). *Love Them or Lose Them: How to Keep Your People Competent*. Wiley.

Kraut, J. (2024). *7 steps to financial freedom: A simple easy to execute strategy to create your financial freedom!* DRES Media.

Sethi, R. (2009). *I Will Teach You to Be Rich: No Guilt. No Excuses. Just a 6-Week Program That Works* (Second Edition). Workman Publishing.

Ziglar, Z. (2000). *Over the top*. Thomas Nelson.

# 7

# PRAGMATISM VS. SUPERFICIALITY

THE SEVENTH AND FINAL MAJOR TRAIT I HAVE OBSERVED among successful individuals is *pragmatism*. Pragmatism is an awareness of what truly matters and the ability to focus on those priorities without being distracted by frills, emotions, or excessive theorizing. When I discuss pragmatism, most people envision great historical figures such as Julius Caesar, Peter the Great, or contemporary figures like Elon Musk or Mark Zuckerberg. Some associate pragmatism with the American spirit.

Whether you view pragmatism as a positive or negative trait, I've found that success in life is extremely difficult to attain without a balanced approach to it. Like the other six traits we've already explored, cultivating healthy pragmatism is essential. In this chapter, we will examine the meaning of pragmatism, its benefits, and how to develop it in our lives.

We will also delve into *superficiality*, the intrinsic temptation that often afflicts pragmatic people. Haste and the absence of non-negotiable values can lead to disastrous consequences for the pragmatic individual. Finally, I will provide suggestions on how to nurture pragmatism and counter the risks of superficiality.

## What Is Pragmatism?

At its core, pragmatism is a practical philosophy that contrasts sharply with idealism.[46] The pragmatist is not an idealist; in fact, he often despises philosophers who offer solutions to non-existent problems. I've found that many people are prone to idealism. This shows up in our conversations through phrases like "it would be great if," "someone should," and "if someone wanted to." Some of us are driven by dissatisfaction and idealism, imagining how things "should" be while feeling overwhelmed by the harsh realities of life.

---

*Pragmatism means solving problems or accomplishing as much as possible with mineral resources.*

---

Pragmatism, on the other hand, is about action; it's about getting things done and making the most out of what we have. The word itself comes from the Greek *pragma,* meaning "action." According to *Webster's Dictionary,* something is pragmatic if it refers to practical matters, often to the exclusion of intellectual or artistic considerations. It's about the practical rather than the idealistic.

Pragmatism draws its philosophical roots from empiricism. The German philosopher Immanuel Kant used the term *pragmatisch* to describe "experiential, empirical, and purposive thinking based on and applied to experience." In early 20th-century America, pragmatism gained popularity based on the idea that the value of ideas is determined by their usefulness and practicability. It's about solving problems or accomplishing as much as possible with minimal resources, being efficient and optimizing every resource.

Pragmatic individuals are not concerned with philosophy or motivation. Instead, they take a direct path toward success through action. Their thinking and activities are fueled by an intuitive sense

[46] Putnam, H. (1994). *Pragmatism.* Blackwell Publishers.

of what matters and what doesn't. The pragmatist sees reality for what it is, recognizes its imperfections, and says, "Never mind! I'll do my best to make the best of every circumstance and every resource, no matter the shortcomings." He believes that things will work out and that he will succeed, regardless of how challenging the situation may be. Pragmatism can be a key trait that contributes to long-term success.

## What Does Pragmatism Look Like?

### *1. Action*[47]

The first manifestation of pragmatism, then, is action itself. Pragmatists prioritize practical results and seek quick solutions. They focus on what can be done now, tackling problems directly, even if the solutions aren't perfect. Rather than becoming bogged down in abstract thinking or waiting for ideal conditions, a pragmatic person adapts quickly to changing circumstances and takes immediate action to achieve their goals. Progress, for the pragmatist, comes from action, learning from experience, and adjusting as needed. This action-oriented approach ensures constant movement, yielding productivity, and tangible results.

The pragmatic person is not concerned with impossible ideals. Instead, he exploits the available resources. Action distinguishes the pragmatist from the philosopher, who might sit, meditate, read, or debate. The pragmatist rolls up his sleeves and begins working to change the world.

### *2. Realism*

Pragmatic individuals see the world as it is and base their decisions on reality. They don't complain or indulge in unattainable ideals or

---

[47] Rorty, R. (1982). *Consequences of pragmatism: Essays, 1972–1980*. University of Minnesota Press.

dreams. Pragmatists understand the limitations of their circumstances and adjust their expectations accordingly. In life, especially in extreme situations, people are often forced to choose between bad and worse options. Consider a war in which the choices may not be between good and bad but rather between bad and terrible. The realist, grounded in pragmatism, has the clarity to choose the lesser evil.

*The pragmatic man is not concerned with impossible ideals – he exploits available resources.*

### *3. Haste*

Pragmatic individuals don't tolerate useless discussions, fanciful stories, or speculative debates. They dislike meetings that conclude with vague phrases like "we'll talk about it next time" or "let's revisit this later." Driven by results, the pragmatist makes swift decisions and immediately implements them rather than wasting time analyzing every detail or seeking perfection. When time is of the essence, the pragmatist moves quickly to find solutions, ensuring that opportunities aren't missed.

Abraham Lincoln serves as a prime example. Lincoln was known for his strong work ethic and dedication to solving problems efficiently. He often held long, standing meetings with his advisors and cabinet members, particularly during the Civil War. He believed that quick, decisive action was essential in times of crisis. One notable example was how he invited his cabinet members into his office without formalities and often stood during meetings, allowing for shorter, more focused discussions. This approach kept meetings centered on the key issues at hand and avoided unnecessary delays.

### *4. Emotional Detachment*

Pragmatic individuals know how to separate themselves from emotionally charged situations. They seem almost immune to criticism, insults, or setbacks that would derail others. If they make a mistake or lose something valuable, they have the resilience to move on without being emotionally devastated. People often describe them as cold-blooded. From my observations, pragmatic individuals who excel at managing their emotions know how to channel emotional pain into productive action. They might express their frustration or discomfort with a statement like, "I'm about to lose it, but I'll push through anyway!" This reflects a mindset of acknowledging the emotional challenges they face but choosing to move forward despite them. They understand that emotional struggles are a part of life, but rather than being consumed by them, they focus on progress and resilience. It's a way of saying, "Yes, this is hard, but I'm not letting it stop me." This practical approach allows them to stay focused on their goals even when emotions could easily derail them.

### *5. Passion*

Passion is the fuel that drives pragmatic work. It is seen in the determination to find solutions, make things work, and overcome obstacles. Pragmatists remain focused on reality, but that doesn't mean they lack enthusiasm. Rather, they channel their passion toward tangible, lasting results. Passion is like the speed of a bicycle: when it slows down too much, the bike falls over even if it's still functional. I've encountered many capable individuals who have lost their passion, becoming immobilized and incapable of action.

### *6. Practicality*

Pragmatic people focus on solutions that can be applied immediately and yield concrete results as quickly as possible. Rather than getting lost in theory or chasing unattainable ideals, the pragmatist prefers to act efficiently, using the resources and information at hand. Every action must have a clear purpose and bring real benefits, avoiding time and energy spent on things that don't contribute directly to achieving goals.

## The Benefits of Pragmatism

### *1. Pragmatism solves problems,[48] whereas idealism merely identifies them.*

Pragmatism emphasizes solutions that work in real-life situations, focusing on practical application rather than theoretical speculation. Pragmatists tackle complex problems by breaking them down into manageable steps, steadily working toward the desired outcome.

### *2. Pragmatism generates results.*

Pragmatic individuals shift their focus from unattainable ideals to achievable, effective goals. They avoid unnecessary complications, ensuring that time and resources are spent on actions that lead to concrete results rather than being trapped in a cycle of unattainable dreams.

### *3. Pragmatism boosts productivity.*

By focusing on what works, pragmatic people improve efficiency, allowing individuals and teams to stay focused on their goals. In some organizations, the absence of clear productivity standards can lead to similar issues, such as suspicion of laziness, inefficiency, and a lack of accountability among employees. Without measurable goals or expectations, employees may feel uncertain about what's required of them, which can foster an environment of mistrust. This

---

[48] McKee, A., Grant, H., Achor, S., & Saunders, E. G. (2022). *Energy + motivation* (HBR Emotional Intelligence Series). Harvard Business Press.

lack of clarity can quickly breed a toxic culture in which workers are less motivated to perform at their best, and management may struggle to hold such teams accountable. The result is a cycle of decreased productivity and morale, with everyone potentially working harder to conceal perceived gaps in effort rather than focusing on delivering results.

### *4. Pragmatism reduces fatigue and increases energy.*

By prioritizing practical solutions over endless analysis or debate, pragmatism simplifies decision-making, enabling quick, effective choices. This is crucial in high-pressure situations in which decisions can significantly impact business outcomes. Leaders, in particular, need this skill to navigate the constant demands of decision-making without succumbing to indecision.

A pragmatist is rarely someone you'll find philosophizing about how the world should be. More often, they're at work, actively engaged in creating the changes they want to see. Their consistent action leads to exponential, long-term impact. Regardless of personality, experience, or preferences, those who wish to succeed in life must learn to master pragmatism.

Of course, pragmatism isn't without its temptations. In the next section, we'll explore the dangers that come with it.

## Superficiality: The Temptation of Pragmatism

As mentioned at the beginning of the chapter, pragmatism is not always a virtue. It is usually accompanied by the danger of superficiality—that is, acting without considering the implications, morality, or deeper meanings of actions.[49] The risk of pragmatism is that it prioritizes action over doctrine or philosophy. Many pragmatists believe they don't need a guiding life philosophy or that they can

[49] Bruch, H., & Ghoshal, S. (2002). Beware the busy manager. *Harvard Business Review, 80*(2), 62–69.

change it depending on the circumstances. Some pragmatists even feel ashamed of their life's goals and values, not fully recognizing what motivates them or what they are pursuing.

Pragmatism often aligns with utility, the belief that only things that work or deliver results are valuable. Just because something works in the immediate term doesn't mean it is ethical or beneficial. History is filled with pragmatic movements that, while producing short-term results or benefiting a minority, led to horrendous atrocities (i.e., wars, pogroms, and atrocities committed in the name of "cleansing" humanity of perceived threats). Pragmatic decisions, when guided solely by expediency, have often resulted in hell on earth.

In truth, each of us operates according to a doctrine of life, whether consciously formulated or not. Every action we take is influenced by a set of beliefs or mental frameworks that operate with or without our awareness.

Pragmatists are often characterized by optimism, a belief that things will work out, that they can make lemonade from the sour lemons of life. Yet this same optimism can blind them, turning their approach into a superficial one. They may act without thinking or adjust their principles based on ever-changing circumstances. Pragmatism can justify selfishness, unethical behavior, and even criminal activity under the guise of "having no choice" or intending to do things differently next time.

## What Is Superficiality?

A superficial person is someone who addresses problems without examining them deeply, skims the surface, and lacks depth. In contrast, a philosopher digs deep into thoughts and analysis, sometimes getting lost in them as though stuck in a swamp. The pragmatist, however, either doesn't notice the swamp or doesn't care about it. His pragmatism and past successes give him a blind belief that he can navigate any challenge without careful consideration. As with the other traits we've discussed, pragmatism is influenced by genetic factors. Some individuals are naturally more detached, can cope more easily with negative experiences, and are innately efficient. The pragmatic individual is rarely bothered by the same frustrations as others. He might say, "So what if he's upset?"; "Why cry?"; "There's no reason to be offended"; or "What are you, a wimp?"

Moreover, superficiality often involves avoiding unpleasant subjects or situations that require emotional involvement. For example, consider some of the immigrants who came to the United States. Many crossed the border with little more than hope for a better future and the determination to work hard, regardless of the type of job available. They often began by taking up low-paying, labor-intensive jobs such as in agriculture, construction, or food service. Despite facing language barriers, discrimination, and sometimes exploitation, they persevered, working long hours without complaint. Over time, many of these immigrant families achieved financial stability and provided their children with access to education and opportunities that allowed the next generation to thrive in ways their parents could only dream of.

But imagine the complications that arise when these parents interact with their American-born children, who are accustomed to American sentimentality and openness and who have not experienced such hardships. The children often accuse their parents of being superficial, claiming they don't understand their emotions or frustrations and that they change their principles according to the situation. Similarly, this dynamic can be observed between employers and employees, especially when employees seek to engage in deep emotional discussions that pragmatists find unnecessary.

Even if a pragmatist has a justification, he doesn't value attention to detail or an in-depth understanding of situations or principles. He tends to focus on appearances—the outward aspects of a situation—without delving into its substance or complexities. In interactions, overemphasis on appearances can result in judgments based on first impressions rather than understanding people more deeply. Superficiality in behavior and speech often manifests as a rushed approach, with little regard for details or long-term consequences.

## What Does Superficiality Look Like?

Superficiality can manifest in many forms, such as hasty judgments, lack of attention to detail, focus primarily on appearances, banal communication, avoidance of serious commitments, and oversimplification of issues. Let's explore some manifestations of superficiality.

### *1. Hurry*

People in a hurry resemble ants; they have little patience for anything. When you try to talk to them, they interrupt mid-sentence. They're always looking for quick, simple solutions without considering the implications. Whether driven by the desire for immediate results or to avoid the discomfort of difficult conversations, they make hasty and superficial decisions. Their hurry might reflect a lack of interest in deeper matters or a fear of becoming emotionally involved in complex situations. They prefer moving quickly from one task to another, sidestepping real engagement.

While often an asset for successful people, this rush can become a liability. There's a fine line between efficiently completing tasks and rushing through them without regard for quality. The pragmatic, hurried person risks being manipulated and deceived. For instance, people know that a superficial boss doesn't read reports carefully, so they might hand her documents riddled with mistakes. Haste and superficiality can also alienate friends, colleagues, and family who might feel like just another task on the to-do list.

### *2. False Values*

Shallow people often place too much importance on public opinion. They are easily influenced by seemingly functional models from others.[50] Instead of taking the time to think critically or analyze a situation, they mimic what seems to work for others.

A painful example from Romania involves the proliferation of casinos and gambling establishments. While banks, pharmacies, and grocery stores go bankrupt, casinos seem to flourish. A pragmatic person looking for a profitable business might consider opening a casino or investing in cryptocurrencies without considering the moral implications or long-term sustainability. They focus on short-term gains, following a model that appears successful without reflecting on its ethical consequences.

### *3. Shifting Values to Fit the Context and Circumstances*

The pragmatist doesn't believe in a universal set of values but instead adopts a "chameleon principle." They act one way with family, another with friends, another at work, and yet another at social events. This can make them unreliable. A person who seemed trustworthy one week may suddenly lack consistency. Pragmatic people with shifting values often say, "Wait and see," or "It depends," leaving others unsure of where they stand. Over time, this behavior erodes trust, and the pragmatist becomes known as unreliable.

### *4. False Priorities*

The most important things in life are our soul, our health, our relationships—especially family relationships—and then, last, our possessions. If we neglect our soul, everything else falls out of balance. If we neglect our health, we'll pay for it later. If we ignore our family, we may find ourselves wealthy but lonely.

In the past two decades, millions of people from various countries have moved abroad in search of better opportunities, and the United States and Western Europe have been primary destinations

[50] Welch, E. T. (2023). *When people are big and God is small: Overcoming peer pressure, codependency, and the fear of man*. New Growth Press.

for many. While I fully understand the drive to provide a better life, having family members—two brothers and three sisters—who have made the U.S. their home, I've observed a concerning trend. Some immigrants, in their pursuit of financial success, end up neglecting their emotional well-being, health, or family connections. The most heartbreaking situations often involve parents who leave their children behind, relying on extended family or technology to take on the parenting role. In some cases, there's a misplaced belief that material possessions—such as expensive clothes, a new car, or the latest smartphone—hold more value than spending quality time with their children, leading to missed opportunities for building deep family bonds. Healthy priorities always involve taking care of our soul, our health, and our family. Only when we order these priorities correctly can we truly experience fulfillment. We can achieve great wealth and success, but if we lose our health or family, all we've gained will mean nothing.

## The Effects of Superficiality

Without careful consideration of what is worth investing time and effort into, a shallow person may experience failure in both their professional and personal life.

### *1. Poor Decisions*

Superficial people "spend money they don't have to buy things they don't need to impress people they don't like."[51]

### *2. Shallow Relationships*

If you're superficial, you may think you have real friends, but they may just be using you. You may believe you have someone to turn

---

[51] Atrr. To Ramsey, D. (2009). *The total money makeover: A proven plan for financial fitness*. Thomas Nelson.

to in times of difficulty, but eventually, you'll realize you're surrounded by opportunists. History has shown that pragmatists often surround themselves with shallow people who ultimately betray them for a better offer.

### *3. Lack of Trust*

Initially, they may be seen as problem-solvers, appreciated for their hard work and practical thinking. But, as time goes on, people start to notice the shallowness of their decisions. They begin to say things like, "They say a lot but do little," or "They promise much but deliver little." This undermines trust. In time, the superficial pragmatist finds themselves isolated, unable to regain the trust of those around them.

## Accountability: The Solution Against Superficiality

To be successful in life and excel as problem-solvers, we must develop a practical and pragmatic mindset. If we are naturally gifted with pragmatism, it's important to recognize how to use this gift for the benefit of others. However, we must be vigilant not to let this natural pragmatism devolve into destructive superficiality.

Being pragmatic is an admirable quality. A person who moves quickly, gets things done, and is involved in a variety of activities is valuable. He's effective in his work and doesn't waste time on trivial matters. In analyzing the dangers faced by pragmatic people, I'm not suggesting we abandon pragmatism. Rather, we must remain alert to its intrinsic risks. The solution I've experienced and witnessed in others who embrace pragmatism is *vigilance*.

Accountability has a primarily spiritual significance. It refers to that heightened state of awareness in which we are alert to potential dangers and take care not to fall into traps. An accountable person stands in stark contrast to one who is inattentive, indifferent, or distracted, believing that everything will resolve itself without effort or attention. I've noticed that many young pragmatists, when confronted with a watchful or cautious attitude, often dismiss it as being petty or out of touch, assuming it merely spoils their joy. The wise King Solomon admonishes us,

> Above all else, guard your heart, for everything you do flows from it. (Prov. 4:23)

## How Can We Cultivate Accountability?

### *1. Soul Reflection*

This involves pausing, reflecting on, and engaging in a conversation with your own soul. For me, reflection is most effective through writing. Others may benefit from having a confessor or mentor to guide their thoughts. Regardless of the method, the key is to learn how to stop the relentless rush of life. Even the most pragmatic people need a sabbath, a moment of stillness. Without this pause, you'll keep running but won't have the opportunity to reflect on what truly matters. It's like embarking on a road trip and wishing to take in the scenery but going at blinding speed; you won't see the beauty of nature, as it will all blur by as you focus only on not crashing. If you slow down, your mind will clear, your vision will sharpen, and your attention can shift to the deeper aspects of life.

A story from Soviet times illustrates this principle. After the Communists took power, a priest suspected of being a Tsarist was placed under the supervision of a young soldier. One morning, the priest went out to fetch water, and the soldier, startled, raised his rifle and shouted, "Wait, who are you? What do you want? Who do you serve? Where are you going?"

The wise priest smiled and calmly responded, "Young Man, I ask that you come to me every morning with that same rifle and ask me the same questions so that I can better understand my purpose in life!"

Sometimes we all need a soldier with a rifle to ask us questions like these: Who are you? What do you want from life? Who do you serve? And where are you going?

### *2. Reflect on Relationships*

Once we've reflected on our own soul, it's crucial to consider our relationships, particularly with our family. Are we truly taking care of them? How is our relationship with our spouse? With our children? With our parents and siblings? Family relationships are foundational, and we cannot afford to neglect them. Many families fall apart when those involved fail to nurture these relationships. Being overly consumed with work, thinking we're providing for our family, is a recipe for disaster. Some people justify their long hours by claiming they are working for the well-being of their family, yet they neglect their children emotionally and miss important moments in their lives—first parties, first loves, first exams, etc.—because they're too busy. If we focus solely on material gain, we will fail to recognize the irreplaceable value of our soul and our family.

I dedicate one day a week, usually Sunday, to reflection and family time. It's a day when I focus on my soul and my family. Even modern science underscores the importance of rest and reflection for innovation and creativity as well as for fostering healthy relationships both at home and at work.[52] Reflection, as I see it, is the conscious act of pausing and detaching to realize what truly matters and what doesn't. It's exactly what pragmatism needs to stay constructive and balanced.

---

[52] Davidson, O. B., Eden, D., Westman, M., Cohen-Charash, Y., Hammer, L. B., Kluger, A. N., Krausz, M., ... & Sharar, E. (2010). Sabbatical leave: Who gains and how much? *Journal of Applied Psychology, 95*(5), 953–964. https://doi.org/10.1037/a0020135.

### *3. Honesty in Communication*

As I've noted before, I've found that many people engage in self-deception. This self-deception is often driven by poor communication—whether evasive, convoluted, or downright false. Honest communication is challenging. It takes time, requires confrontation, and often makes us feel uncomfortable or inadequate. We may believe that everything is going well and everyone is happy, but honest communication reveals the truth.

In many corporations, there's a principle of objective reporting based on performance indicators. Periodically, every company produces a financial report to provide a true picture of its situation. In business, we do this because we understand human subjectivity. If you ask any boss, they'll likely believe their company is doing well. Likewise, employees often think their work is exemplary. To test these assumptions, we need objective reporting and honest communication. Without it, we risk misjudging our progress. Having life goals, periodic evaluations, and honest assessments is essential for ensuring we're on the right track. The key is having the courage to speak honestly and transparently and to establish mechanisms for evaluation and reporting.

### *4. Mentors*

We should surround ourselves with amazing mentors. These mentors should be mature individuals who encourage, motivate, and guide us, helping us stay on course and correcting us when necessary. Mentors can be people from the past whose works and biographies inspire us. I recommend seeking mentors who are close to you—even if they are imperfect—but who truly know you, want you to succeed, and can provide honest, objective feedback.

In comparing large corporations with smaller firms that struggle to survive, one noticeable difference is the presence of an oversight body—a board of directors—that holds managers and employees accountable. In successful organizations, there's a healthy system of accountability[53] that ensures people stay on track and meet their goals.

### *5. Cultivating Good Friendships*

St. Paul wisely wrote, "Do not be misled: 'Bad company corrupts good character'"(1 Cor. 15:33). By extension, good friendships foster good habits. The friends we choose and the colleagues with whom we work play crucial roles in our success. Friends who share our values, encourage us, and hold us accountable are invaluable. Unfortunately, many of us maintain friendships merely to feel good rather than to grow. While it's essential to enjoy the company of friends, if they don't make you better, it's time to reconsider those relationships. A healthy friendship is one in which both people watch over each other, encouraging one another to love and do good.

---

*The most common danger of people who want success is to limit themselves to material possessions.*

---

[53] Kose, J., & Senbet, L. W. (1998). Corporate governance and board effectiveness. *Journal of Banking & Finance*, 22(4), 371–403. https://doi.org/10.1016/S0378-4266(98)00005-3.

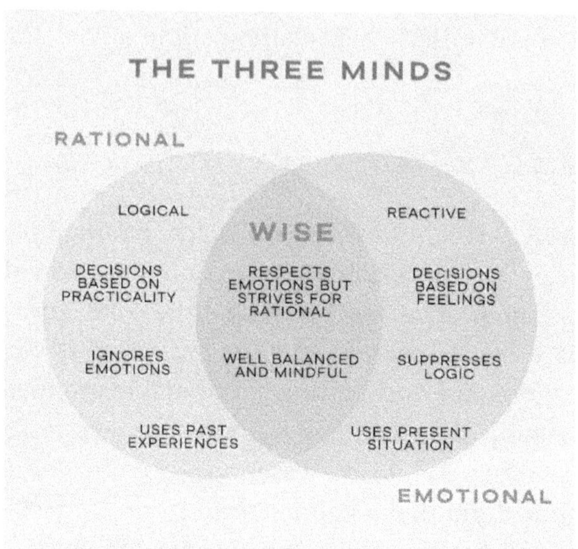


I've shared examples of how unchecked pragmatism has led to tragedies and even atrocities, but I want to conclude this chapter with the story of one of my heroes, 19th-century British parliamentarian William Wilberforce, who played a pivotal role in the abolition of slavery within the British Empire. Wilberforce epitomizes the power of pragmatism when it is guided by noble ideals. In 1780, at just 21 years old, he was elected to the British Parliament as its youngest member. At the time, the wealth of the British Empire was built on slavery, a practice borrowed from the Spanish, who had adopted it from Africa. Wilberforce's mentor was John Newton, a former captain of a slave-trading ship.

For a time, Wilberforce contemplated retiring from politics. But his friend, the young prime minister William Pitt, reminded him that the principles of Christianity call not only for meditation but for action. After reflecting, Wilberforce chose to stay in Parliament and dedicate his life to two causes: the abolition of the slave trade and the reform of society's morals. Throughout his career, he invested his time, wealth, and health—never losing focus on his mission. Despite his busy political life, Wilberforce never neglected his faith. His Christian beliefs were his shield and anchor. In addition, he remained a devoted family man, nurturing strong relationships with his wife and children.

Wilberforce's efforts were not in vain. His determination and pragmatism eventually led to the abolition of the slave trade and substantial social reform in Britain. His example shows how pragmatism, when harnessed for a noble cause, can lead to profound and lasting change.

## Reflection and Discussion

*1. Where do I see this strength—and its shadow—in my own life?*

*2. What situations most often trigger the temptation connected to this strength?*

*3. What safeguards or disciplines can I put in place to cultivate the strength while resisting its temptation?*

*4. Who in my life models this strength well, and what can I learn from their example?*

# Further Reading

Bartlett, S. (2021). *Diary of a CEO: 33 laws of success in life and business*. Piatkus.

Blanchard, K., & Johnson, S. (1985). *The new manager by the minute*. Berkley Books.

Brantley, J., Wood, J. C., & McKay, M. (2017). *How to manage your overwhelming emotions and regain self-control: The dialectical behavior therapy practical guide*. New Harbinger Publications.

Cardone, G. (2011). *The 10X rule: The only difference between success and failure*. Wiley.

Collins, J. (2001). *Good to great: Why some companies make the leap… and others don't*. Harper Business.

Hill, N. (1928). *The law of success: The master course*. The Ralston Society.

Lencioni, P. (1998). *The five temptations of a CEO: A business classic*. Jossey-Bass.

Mate, G. (2003). *When the body says no: The cost of hidden stress*. Wiley.

McKeown, G. (2011). *Essentialism: The discipline of pursuing less*. Crown Business.

Peale, N. V. (1952). *The power of positive thinking*. Prentice Hall.

Tate, C. (2013). *Work effectively*. The Tate Group.

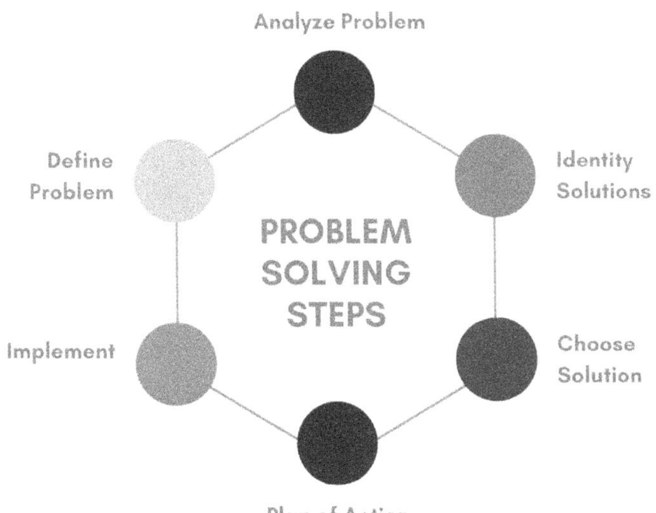
Analyze Problem
Define
Problem
Identity
Solutions
PROBLEM
SOLVING
STEPS
Implement
Choose
Solution
Plan of Action

# CONCLUSION

SUCCESS IS A UNIVERSAL DESIRE. I HAVE YET TO MEET anyone who consciously and seriously wishes to be a failure. Unfortunately, however, I have encountered many people who possess a mistaken understanding of success or believe there is a single element (e.g., money) that defines it. Success is deeply individualized and depends on one's context and circumstances. Each of us is shaped by unique experiences, and each has a different key to unlocking their own version of success. What fulfills me will not necessarily fulfill you, and the projects for which I am gifted may not suit or appeal to you. However, there are universally valid elements I believe constitute success.

Success encompasses an element of material wealth, which is necessary for daily living. The most common pitfall for those who seek success is the tendency to limit it to the acquisition of material possessions. While material resources are important, success also involves earning respect and influence, the ability to contribute positively to others' lives, and improve society.

Another component of success is harmony within one's family and community. But all of this must be built on inner peace, which I believe is the most essential element of success. One can achieve success even without influence or material resources if they possess inner peace and family harmony.

Over the past 30 years of study and observation, I have identified seven traits that successful people possess, along with seven temptations or pitfalls associated with these traits. The message of this book is to acquire and cultivate these traits to achieve success. However, I also warn against the inherent temptations that success can bring, offering solutions to neutralize them.

## 1. Natural Talents

The first trait I refer to is natural talents, those innate qualities such as energy, intelligence, memory, charisma, and courage. These are the gifts we are born with that reside in our DNA, independent of any effort on our part. Natural talents also include experiences or opportunities such as the family we are born into, the education we receive, or the chance to travel and learn foreign languages. These are things we may not have cultivated ourselves, but they shape our lives, and we have the choice to respond to them either constructively or destructively.

The temptation associated with natural talents is pride. People who take credit for things they didn't accomplish or who have overcome significant hardships are often tempted to boast. When success leads to measurable results, accompanied by public recognition, the temptation to develop a sense of superiority arises. Pride can hinder personal growth and alienate us from friends and family, instilling a spirit of contempt for those who do not share our gifts or experiences.

To combat pride, it's crucial to recognize that we are not the ultimate owners of our gifts; we are stewards. Everything we possess is a gift, and we have a responsibility to a supportive community. To master pride, we must cultivate humble altruism, using our gifts for the benefit of others. Who we are is far more important than what we do or what we have.

## 2. Persuasiveness

The second trait is persuasiveness. Persuasive negotiators are often pragmatic, know the importance of preparation, understand the power of persuasion, are attuned to others' preferences, and know how to control their emotions. Regardless of innate qualities, negotiation skills can be cultivated because, in life, we don't always get what we deserve; we get what we negotiate.

The temptation for persuasive negotiators is lying, which often begins with self-deception. We justify small lies to ourselves, telling ourselves that everyone lies or that the consequences are minimal. However, lying can damage mental health, diminish self-confidence, and destroy reputations.

To counteract the temptation to lie, we must take responsibility for our actions and be willing to accept short-term losses to preserve our integrity. We should focus on character, reputation, and long-term success.

## 3. Industriousness

The third trait is industriousness, embodied in honesty and hard work. An industrious and hard-working person does their best even when they don't feel like it. Industriousness requires personal sacrifice, discipline, and the ability to produce quality work without supervision. The industrious person is discerning, knows when to say "no," and understands the value of teamwork and delegation. While hard work can sometimes be underappreciated, it always pays off in the long run, building experience, skills, and opportunities.

The temptation that comes with industriousness and hard work is materialism, the pursuit of material possessions to fulfill spiritual or emotional needs. Materialism leads us to prioritize things over character, relationships, and inner peace. It becomes dangerous when we seek material things dishonestly or without hard work.

The antidote to materialism is altruism, rooted in the Christian principle that "it is more blessed to give than to receive." Altruism requires transparency, discipline, and generosity in both thought and action. It helps us remain grounded and focused on what truly matters.

## 4. Creativity

The fourth trait is creativity, which is defined not merely by inventiveness but by the ability to solve problems in innovative ways.

Creative people possess adaptability, ingenuity, vision, optimism, problem-solving skills, and leadership. They are forward-thinking and involved in their work, constantly looking for ways to improve and lead others.

The temptation for creative individuals is destructive dissatisfaction. Rather than channeling their creativity into constructive problem-solving, they may become overly critical, frustrated, or cynical. This discontent can paralyze them, preventing them from seizing opportunities and poisoning their relationships.

The solution is to embrace loss as a natural part of the journey, seeing it as a lesson rather than a setback. Recognize that failure can lead to growth and focus on long-term success rather than short-term perfection.

## 5. Determination

The fifth trait is determination, the unwavering will to pursue one's goals despite obstacles. Determined people are resilient, overcoming setbacks with reason and perseverance. Determination involves hard work, consistency, and the ability to move forward despite fatigue, rejection, or disappointment. It is fueled by logic and a deep belief in the value of one's goals.

Unfortunately, determination can be tempting to pair with anger. Angry people may lash out recklessly or develop a cynical attitude. Anger leads to poor decisions, damaged reputations, and strained relationships.

The solution to anger is to view life as a series of lessons and challenges to be overcome, trusting that setbacks can ultimately help us grow. Faith in a higher purpose, the belief that negative experiences can turn into valuable lessons, can provide peace and guidance in moments of frustration.

## 6. Altruism

The sixth trait is altruism, which is characterized by the generosity of spirit and the principle of "earn as much as you can, save as much as you can, and give as much as you can." Altruistic individuals understand the importance of investing in others and fostering relationships based on sincerity and mutual benefit.

The temptation faced by altruistic people is revenge. After being betrayed or manipulated, they may become disillusioned and develop a sense of entitlement or desire for payback. This can lead to resentment, envy, and deep distrust of others, ultimately damaging relationships and personal well-being.

The solution is to leave vengeance to God, trusting that divine justice will prevail. Forgiveness, a central tenet of Christian teaching, offers a path to healing and restoration, freeing us from the burden of anger and bitterness.

## 7. Pragmatism

The final trait of successful people is pragmatism, an approach that is realistic, action-oriented, and grounded in the practicalities of life. Pragmatic individuals make decisions based on what will work in the real world, understanding that life often involves choosing between imperfect options. Pragmatism is about generating results, overcoming obstacles, and making the best of every situation.

The temptation of pragmatism is superficiality, the tendency to address problems hastily or without considering their long-term implications. Superficiality leads to poor judgment, a lack of depth, and a focus on appearances rather than substance.

To counteract this, we must practice vigilance, periodically reassessing our actions and ensuring they align with our values. Cultivating relationships with true friends and mentors who value character over external success is key to maintaining depth and integrity in our decisions.

## Summary of Success Traits, Temptations, and Solutions

| Trait | Temptation | Solution |
|---|---|---|
| Natural Endowments | Pride | Awareness |
| Persuasiveness | Deception | Taking responsibility |
| Industriousness | Materialism | Sustainable altruism |
| Creativity | Destructive dissatisfaction | Embracing loss |
| Determination | Anger | Heavenly reward |
| Altruism | Revenge | Divine vengeance |
| Pragmatism | Superficiality | Watchfulness |

I hope this book has helped you understand the traits of successful people. Due to constraints of time and space, I have focused on presenting the essential elements of these topics, offering sufficient analysis for you to understand and apply them in your daily life. I also highlighted the intrinsic temptations that accompany these traits, hoping you will be able to master them on your journey to success. May you find success and blessings from above.

I leave you with the motto of my life:

> "Do not be overcome by evil but overcome evil with good" (Rom. 12:21).

# REFERENCES


Abdaal, A. (2023). *Feel-good productivity: How to achieve more of what matters to you*. Ebury Edge.

Acemoglu, D., & Robinson, J. A. (2012). *Why nations fail: The origins of power, prosperity, and poverty*. Crown Business.

Allen, D. (2001). *Getting things done: The art of stress-free productivity*. Penguin Books.

Antonakis, J., Fenley, M., & Liechti, S. (2012). Learning charisma: Transform yourself into the person others want to follow. *Harvard Business Review, 90*(6), 127–130.

Ariely, D., & Jones, S. (2012). *The honest truth about dishonesty: How we lie to everyone—especially ourselves*. HarperCollins.

Arnold, C. L. (2013). *Small steps, big changes: A breakthrough program to transform your life with a single action*. Wiley.

Arteaga, R., & Hyland, J. (2013). *Pivot: How top entrepreneurs adapt and change course to find ultimate success*. Wiley.

Barringer, B. R., & Ireland, R. D. (2015). *Entrepreneurship: Successfully launching new ventures* (5th ed.). Pearson.

Beattie, H. J. (2005). Revenge. *Journal of the American Psychoanalytic Association, 53*(2), 513–524. https://doi.org/10.1177/000306510505300206.

Brand, P., & Yancey, P. (2014). *A disease so strange: A novel*. Tyndale House Publishers.

Bufford, B. (1994). *Halftime: Moving from success to significance*. Zondervan.

Burkett, L. (2006). *Business by the book: The complete guide of biblical principles for the workplace*. Thomas Nelson.

Carnegie, D. (2005). *The secret of success*. National Book Network.

Carnegie, D. (2009). *How to win friends and influence people*. Simon & Schuster.

Carnegie & Associates, D. (2019). *Sell!: The way your customers want to buy*. G&D Media.

Carnegie Training, D. (2011). *Stand and deliver: How to become a masterful communicator and public speaker*. Simon & Schuster.

Christensen, C. M. (1997). *The innovator's dilemma: When new technologies cause great firms to fail*. Harvard Business School Press.

Clason, G. S. (2008). *The richest man in Babylon*. Signet.

Clear, J. (2018). *Atomic habits: Tiny changes, remarkable results: An easy & proven way to build good habits & break bad ones*. Avery.

Cloud, H. (2023). *Trust: Knowing when to give it, when to withhold it, how to earn it, and how to fix it when it gets broken*. Worthy Publishing.

Collins, J., & Lazier, B. (2020). *BE 2.0 (Beyond Entrepreneurship 2.0): Turning your business into an enduring great company*. Portfolio.

Covey, S. R. (2014). *The 7 habits of highly effective people: Interactive edition*. FranklinCovey Co.

Craib, I. (1994). *The importance of disappointment*. Routledge. https://doi.org/10.4324/9780203422236.

Currey, M. (2013). *Daily rituals: How artists work*. Knopf.

Dalio, R. (2017). *Principles: Life and work*. Simon & Schuster.

David, D. (2017). *The psychology of the Roman people: Psychological profiling of the Romans in a cognitive-experimental monograph*. Cambridge Scholars Publishing.

Deci, E. L., & Ryan, R. M. (2012). Self-determination theory. In P. A. Van Lange, A. W.

Dias, D. (2021). *The ten human typologies: Who we are and who we could be*. Routledge.

Donders, P. Ch. (2000). *Kreative Lebensplanung* [Creative life planning]. Gerth Medien GmbH.

Duckworth, A. L., & Gross, J. J. (2014). Self-control and grit: Related but separable determinants of success. *Current Directions in Psychological Science, 23*(5), 319–325. https://doi.org/10.1177/0963721414541462

Duhigg, C. (2016). *Smarter faster better: The secrets of being productive in life and business*. Random House.

Drucker, P. F. (1981). What is "business ethics"? *The Public Interest*, (63), 18–36.

Drucker, P. F. (2004). What makes an effective executive. *Harvard Business Review, 82*(6), 58–63.

# REFERENCES


Drucker, P. F., Collins, J. C., Kotler, P., Kouzes, J. M., Rodin, J., & Rangan, V. K. (2011). *The five most important questions you will ever ask about your organization*. Jossey-Bass.

Eldredge, J. (2001). *Wild at heart: Discovering the secret of a man's soul*. Thomas Nelson.

Foster, R. J. (1998). *Celebration of discipline: The path to spiritual growth* (20th anniversary ed.). HarperSanFrancisco.

Frankl, V. E. (2006). *Man's search for meaning* (I. Lasch, Trans.). Beacon Press. (Original work published 1946)

Goleman, D. (1995). *Emotional intelligence: Why it can matter more than IQ*. Bantam Books.

Guinness, O. (2003). *The call: Finding and fulfilling the central purpose of your life*. Thomas Nelson.

Heath, C., & Heath, D. (2010). *Switch: How to change things when change is hard*. Broadway Books.

Heschel, A. J. (1951). *The Sabbath: Its meaning for modern man*. Farrar, Straus, and Giroux.

Hybels, B. (2002). *Courageous leadership*. Zondervan.

Ingram, C. (2003). *Holy ambition: What it takes to make a difference for God*. Moody Publishers.

Keller, T. (2008). *The reason for God: Belief in an age of skepticism*. Dutton.

Keller, T. (2011). *Counterfeit gods: The empty promises of money, sex, and power, and the only hope that matters*. Riverhead Books.

Keller, T. (2012). *Every good endeavor: Connecting your work to God's work* (with K. Leary Alsdorf). Dutton.

Kruglanski, & E. T. Higgins (Eds.), *Handbook of theories of social psychology* (Vol. 1, pp. 416–436). Sage Publications Ltd.

Lencioni, P. (2002). *The five dysfunctions of a team: A leadership fable*. Jossey-Bass.

Lewis, C. S. (1942). *The Screwtape letters*. Geoffrey Bles.

Lewis, C. S. (1952). *Mere Christianity*. Geoffrey Bles.

Lopez, S. J., & Snyder, C. R. (Eds.). (2011). *The Oxford handbook of positive psychology* (2nd ed.). Oxford University Press.

Maxwell, J. C. (1998). *The 21 irrefutable laws of leadership: Follow them and people will follow you*. Thomas Nelson.

McAdams, D. P. (2006). The redemptive self: Generativity and the stories Americans live by. *Research in Human Development, 3*(2–3), 81–100. https://doi.org/10.1080/15427609.2006.9683363.

Merton, T. (2005). *No man is an island*. Shambhala Publications (Original work published 1955).

Nouwen, H. J. M. (1989). *In the name of Jesus: Reflections on Christian leadership*. Crossroad.

Peterson, J. B. (2018). *12 rules for life: An antidote to chaos*. Random House Canada.

Piper, J. (2003). *Desiring God: Meditations of a Christian Hedonist* (Rev. ed.). Multnomah Publishers.

Scazzero, P. (2006). *Emotionally healthy spirituality: It's impossible to be spiritually mature, while remaining emotionally immature*. Thomas Nelson.

Sinek, S. (2009). *Start with why: How great leaders inspire everyone to take action*. Portfolio.

Stanley, A. (2006). *Visioneering: God's blueprint for developing and maintaining personal vision*. Multnomah Books.

Tutu, D. (2000). *No future without forgiveness*. Image.

Volf, M. (2005). *Free of charge: Giving and forgiving in a culture stripped of grace*. Zondervan.

Warren, R. (2002). *The purpose driven life: What on earth am I here for?* Zondervan.

Willard, D. (1998). *The divine conspiracy: Rediscovering our hidden life in God*. HarperSanFrancisco.

Wright, N. T. (2010). *After you believe: Why Christian character matters*. HarperOne.

Biblical References: The Holy Bible, New International Version. (2011). Zondervan. (Original work published 1973)

www.ingramcontent.com/pod-product-compliance
Ingram Content Group UK Ltd.
Pitfield, Milton Keynes, MK11 3LW, UK
UKHW020424250726
13967UKWH00007B/2803

9 781962 802673